THE J
SINN

CW00542425

THE JERUSALEM SINNER SAVED

OR, GOOD NEWS FOR THE VILEST OF MEN

John Bunyan

'Beginning at Jerusalem' (*Luke* 24:47).

THE BANNER OF TRUTH TRUST

THE BANNER OF TRUTH TRUST
3 Murrayfield Road, Edinburgh EH12 6EL, UK
P.O. Box 621, Carlisle, PA 17013, USA

*

First Published in London, 1691
First Banner of Truth edition, 2005

ISBN 0 85151 914 8

*

Typeset in 10¹/₂/14 pt Sabon at the
Banner of Truth Trust, Edinburgh
Printed in the USA by
Versa Press, Inc.,
East Peoria, IL

Contents

Preface to Offor Edition, 1854[1]

THAT Bunyan, who considered himself one of the most notorious of Jerusalem sinners, should write with the deepest earnestness upon this subject is not surprising. He had preached upon it with very peculiar pleasure, and, doubtless, from many texts, and, as he says, 'through God's grace, with great success'. It is not probable that, with his characteristic intensity of feeling, and holy fervour in preaching, he ever delivered the same sermon twice; but this was a subject so in unison with his own feelings and experience that he must have dilated upon it with even unusual interest and earnestness. The marrow of all these exercises he concentrated in this treatise; and when his judgment was, by severe internal conflicts, fully

[1] The present edition is based on the text in the 3-volume edition of Bunyan's works published in Glasgow in 1854 and edited by George Offor (reprinted Edinburgh: Banner of Truth, 1991; ISBN 0 85151 598 3, the set of three volumes). For the present edition, some of the original language and grammar have been slightly modified to make the work more accessible to present-day readers.

matured – upon the eve of the close of his earthly pilgrimage, in the last year of his life, 1688 – he published it in a pocket volume of eight sheets. It was soon translated into several languages, and became so popular as to pass through ten editions in English by 1728. Like other favourite books it was ornamented with some very inferior wood-cuts.

The object of the author is fully explained in the title to his book. It is to display the riches of divine grace and mercy to the greatest sinners – even to those whose conduct entitled them to be called 'Satan's colonels, and captains, the leaders of his people; and they that most stoutly make head against the Son of God' (p. 34). It is to those who feel themselves to be such, and who make a proper estimate of their own characters, as in the sight of God, that the gracious proclamations of the gospel are peculiarly directed. They to whom much is forgiven love much; and the same native energies which had been misdirected to promote evil, when sanctified and divinely guided, become a great blessing to the church, and to society at large.

Bunyan does not stoop to any attempt to reconcile the humbling doctrines of grace to the self-righteous pride of those who, considering themselves but little sinners, would feel contaminated by the company of those who had been such great sinners, although they were pardoned and sanctified by God. His great effort was directed to relieve the distress and despair of those who were suffering under deep convictions; still, his whole treatise shows that the doctrine of salvation by grace, of free gift, is no encouragement to sin that grace may abound, as some have blasphemously asserted. It is degrading to the pride of those who have not drunk so deeply of sin to be placed upon a level with great sinners. But the disease is the same – in breaking one commandment, the whole law is violated; and, however in some the moral leprosy does not make such fearful ravages as in others, the slightest taint conveys moral, spiritual, and eternal death. All, whether young or old, great or small, must be saved by grace, or fall into perdition. The difference between the taint of sin, and its awfully developed leprosy, is given on pp. 90–1. Who so ready to fly to the physician as those who feel their case to be desperate? and, when cured, they must love the Saviour most.

Comparatively little sins before conviction, when seen in the glass of God's law, and in his holy presence, become great ones. Those who feel themselves to be great sinners, are peculiarly invited to the arms of the Saviour, who saves to the uttermost all that come unto him; and it is thus that peculiar consolation is poured in, and the broken heart is bound up. We are then called by name, as Bunyan forcibly describes it, as men called by name before a court. 'Who first cry out, "Here, sir"; and then shoulder and crowd, and say, "Pray give way, I am called into the court." This is thy case, wherefore say, "Stand away, devil, Christ calls me; stand away, unbelief, Christ calls me; stand away, all my discouraging apprehensions, for my Saviour calls me to him to receive of his mercy."' 'Wherefore, since Christ says come, let the angels make a lane, and let all men give place, that the Jerusalem sinner may come to Jesus Christ for mercy' (p. 75).

How characteristic is this of the peculiarly striking style of Bunyan! How solemn his warnings! The invitations of the gospel will be, to those who refuse them, 'the hottest coals in hell' (p. 78). His reasonings against despair are equally forcible:

''Tis a sin to begin to despair before one sets his foot over the threshold of hell gates ... What! despair of bread in a land that is full of corn! despair of mercy, when our God is full of mercy! when he goes about by his ministers, beseeching of sinners to be reconciled unto him! Thou scrupulous fool, where canst thou find that God was ever false to his promise, or that he ever deceived the soul that ventured itself upon him?' (pp. 81–2).

This whole treatise abounds with strong consolation to those who are beset with fears, and who, because of these, are ready to give way to despair; it ought to be put into the hands of all such, let them belong to what party they may; for, like our author's other books, nothing of a sectarian nature can be traced in it, except we so call the distinguishing truths of evangelical religion. There are some very interesting references to Bunyan's experience and life (pp. 34, 36); and one rather singular idea, in which I heartily concur; it is that the glorified saints will, 'in all likelihood', become part of the heavenly hierarchy of angels and take the places of those who fell from that exalted state (*Rev.* 22:8–9; see p. 95).

To those whose souls are invaded by despair, or who fear that they have committed the sin against the Holy Ghost – to all who pant to have their faith strengthened, and hopes brightened, this little work is most earnestly and affectionately commended.

GEORGE OFFOR
1854

Author's Preface

COURTEOUS READER,

O NE reason which moved me to write and print this little book was because, though there are many excellent heart-affecting discourses in the world that tend to convert the sinner, yet I had a desire to try this simple method of mine; wherefore I make bold thus to invite and encourage the worst to come to Christ for life.

I have been vile myself, but have obtained mercy; and I would have my companions in sin partake of mercy too: and, therefore, I have writ this little book.

The nation doth swarm with vile ones now, as ever it did since it was a nation. My little book, in some places, can scarce go from house to house, but it will find a suitable subject to spend itself upon. Now, since Christ Jesus is willing to save the vilest, why should they not, by name, be somewhat acquainted with it, and bid come to him under that name?

A great sinner, when converted, seems a *booty* to Jesus Christ; he *gets* by saving such an one; why then should both Jesus lose his glory and the sinner lose his soul at once, and that for want of an invitation?

I have found, through God's grace, good success in preaching upon this subject, and, perhaps, so I may by my writing upon it too. I have, as you see, let down this net for a draught. The Lord catch some great fishes by it, for the magnifying of his truth. There are some most vile in all men's eyes, and some are so in their own eyes too; but some have their paintings, to shroud their vileness under; yet they are naked and open unto the eyes of him with whom we have to do; and for all these, God hath sent a Saviour, Jesus; and to all these the door is opened.

Wherefore, pray thee, profane man, give this little book the reading. Come; pardon, and a part in heaven and glory, cannot be hurtful to thee. Let not thy lusts and folly drive thee beyond the door of mercy, since it is not locked nor bolted up against thee. Manasseh was a bad man, and Magdalene a bad woman, to say nothing of the thief upon the cross, or of the murderers of Christ; yet they obtained mercy; Christ willingly received them.

And dost thou think that those, once so bad, now they are in heaven, repent them there because they left their sins for Christ when they were in the world? I cannot believe but that thou thinkest they have verily got the best of it. Why, sinner, do thou likewise. Christ, at heaven's gates, says to thee, Come hither; and the devil, at the gates of hell, does call thee to come to him. Sinner, what sayest thou? Whither wilt thou go? Don't go into the fire; there thou wilt be burned! Don't let Jesus lose his longing, since it is for thy salvation, but come to him and live.

One word more, and so I have done. Sinner, here thou dost hear of love; pray thee, do not provoke it, by turning it into wantonness. He that dies for slighting love, sinks deepest into hell, and will there be tormented by the remembrance of that evil, more than by the deepest cogitation of all his other sins. Take heed, therefore; do not make love thy tormentor, sinner. Farewell.

JOHN BUNYAN
1688

1

The Text Explained

Beginning at Jerusalem (Luke 24:47)

THE whole verse runs thus: 'And that repentance and remission of sins should be preached in his name among all nations, beginning at Jerusalem.' The words were spoken by Christ, after he rose from the dead, and they are here rehearsed after a historical manner, but do contain in them a formal commission, with a special clause therein. The commission is, as you see, for the preaching of the gospel, and is very distinctly inserted in the holy record by Matthew and Mark. 'Go – teach all nations', etc. (*Matt.* 28:19). 'Go ye into all the world, and preach the gospel to every creature' (*Mark* 16:15). Only this clause is specially mentioned by Luke, who says that as Christ would have the doctrine of repentance and remission of sins preached in his name among all nations, so he would have the people of Jerusalem to have the first proffer thereof. Preach it, says Christ, in all nations, but begin at Jerusalem.

The apostles, then, though they had a commission so large as to give them warrant to go and preach the gospel in all the world, yet by this clause they were limited as to the beginning of their ministry; they were to begin this work at Jerusalem. 'Beginning at Jerusalem.'

Before I proceed to an observation upon the words, I must, but briefly, touch upon two things: namely, FIRST, Show you what Jerusalem now was. SECOND, Show you what it was to preach the gospel to them.

FIRST, Jerusalem is to be considered either, *First*, With respect to the descent of her people; or, *Second*, With respect to her preference and exaltation; or, *Third*, With respect to her present state, as to her decays.

First, As to her descent, she was from Abraham, [by] the sons of Jacob, a people that God singled out from the rest of the nations, to set his love upon them.

Secondly, As to her preference or exaltation, she was the place of God's worship, and had in and with her the special tokens and signs of God's favour and presence, above any other people in the world. Hence, the tribes went up to Jerusalem to worship; there was God's house, God's high-priest, God's sacrifices accepted, and God's eye, and God's heart perpetually (*Psa.* 76:1–2; *Psa.* 122; *1 Kings* 9:3). But,

Thirdly, We are to consider Jerusalem also in her decays; for, as she is so considered, she is the proper object of our text, as will be further shown by and by.

Jerusalem, as I told you, was the place and seat of God's worship, but now decayed, degenerated, and apostatized.

The Word, the rule of worship, was rejected of them, and in its place they had put and set up their own traditions: they had rejected, also, the most weighty ordinances, and put in the room thereof their own little things (*Matt.* 15; *Mark* 7). Jerusalem was therefore now greatly back-slidden, and become the place where truth and true religion were much defaced.

It was also now become the very sink of sin and seat of hypocrisy, and the gulf where true religion was drowned. Here also now reigned presumption, and groundless confidence in God, which is the bane of souls. Amongst its rulers, doctors, and leaders, envy, malice, and blasphemy vented themselves against the power of godliness, in all places where it was espied; as also against the promoters of it; yea, their Lord and Maker could not escape them.

In a word, Jerusalem was now become the shambles, the very slaughter-shop for saints. This was the place wherein the prophets, Christ, and his people, were most horribly persecuted and murdered. Yea, so hardened at this time was this Jerusalem in her sins, that she feared not to commit the biggest, and to bind herself, by wish, under the guilt and damning evil of it; saying, when she had murdered the Son of God, 'His blood be on us, and on our children.' And though Jesus Christ did, both by doctrine, miracles, and holiness of life, seek to put a stop to their villainies, yet they shut their eyes, stopped their ears, and rested not, till, as was hinted before, they had driven him out of the world. Yea, that they might, if possible, have extinguished his name, and exploded his doctrine out of the world, they, against all argument, and in despite of heaven, its mighty hand, and undeniable proof of his resurrection, did hire soldiers to invent a lie, saying, his disciples stole him away from the grave; on purpose that men might not count him the Saviour of the world, nor trust in him for the remission of sins.

They were, says Paul, contrary to all men: for they did not only shut up the door of life against themselves, but forbade that it should be opened to any else. 'Forbidding us', says he, 'to speak to the Gentiles, that they might be saved, to fill up their sins alway' (1 *Thess.* 2:14–16; *Matt.* 23:35; 15:7–9; *Mark* 7:6–8; *Matt.* 3:7–9; *John* 8:33, 41; *Matt.* 27:18; *Mark* 3:30; *Matt.* 23:37; *Luke* 13:33–34; *Matt.* 27:25; 20:11–16).

This is the city, and these are the people; this is their character, and these are their sins: nor can there be produced their parallel in all this world. Nay, what world, what people, what nation, for sin and transgression, could or can be compared to Jerusalem? especially if you join to the matter of fact the light they sinned against, and the patience which they abused. Infinite was the wickedness upon this account which they committed.

After all their abusings of wise men, and prophets, God sent unto them John the Baptist, to reduce them, and then his Son, to redeem them; but they would be neither reduced nor redeemed, but persecuted both to the death. Nor did they, as I said, stop here; the holy apostles they afterwards persecuted also to death, even so many as they could; the rest they drove from them unto the utmost corners.

SECOND, I come now to show you what it was to preach the gospel to them. It was, says Luke, to preach to them 'repentance and remission of sins' in Christ's name; or, as Mark has it, to bid them 'repent and believe the gospel' (*Mark* 1:15). Not that repentance is a cause of remission, but a sign of our hearty reception thereof. Repentance is therefore here put to intimate, that no pretended faith of the gospel is good that is not accompanied with it; and this he doth on purpose, because he would not have them deceive themselves: for with what faith can he expect remission of sins in the name of Christ, that is not heartily sorry for them? Or how shall a man be able to give to others a satisfactory account of his unfeigned subjection to the gospel, that yet abides in his impenitency?

Wherefore repentance is here joined with faith, in the way of receiving the gospel. Faith is that without which it cannot be received at all; and repentance that without which it cannot be received unfeignedly. When, therefore, Christ says, he would have repentance and remission of sins preached in his name among all nations, it is as much as to say, I will that all men everywhere be sorry for their sins, and accept of mercy at God's hand through me, lest they fall under his wrath in the judgment; for, as I have said, without repentance, what pretence soever men have of faith, they cannot escape the wrath to come. Wherefore Paul says, God commands 'all men everywhere to repent' (in order to their salvation): 'because he hath appointed a day, in the which he shall judge the world in righteousness by that man whom he hath ordained' (*Acts* 17:31).

And now, to come to this clause, 'Beginning at Jerusalem'; that is, that Christ would have Jerusalem have the first offer of the gospel.

1. This cannot be so commanded because they had now any more right, of themselves, thereto, than had any of the nations of the world; for their sins had divested them of all self-deservings.

2. Nor yet because they stood upon the advance-ground with the worst of the sinners of the nations; nay, rather, the sinners of the nations had the advance-ground of them: for Jerusalem was, long before she had added this iniquity to her sin, worse than the very nations that God cast out before the children of Israel (2 *Chron.* 33:3).

3. It must, therefore, follow, that this clause, 'Beginning at Jerusalem', was put into this commission of mere grace and compassion, even from the overflowings of the bowels of mercy; for indeed they were the worst, and so in the most deplorable condition of any people under the heavens.

Whatever, therefore, their relation was to Abraham, Isaac, or Jacob – however they formerly had been the people among whom God had placed his name and worship, they were now degenerated from God, more than the nations were from their idols, and were become guilty of the highest sins which the people of the world were capable of committing. Nay, none can be capable of committing such *pardonable* sins as they committed against their God, when they slew his Son, and persecuted his name and Word.

From these words, therefore, thus explained, we gain this observation: *That Jesus Christ would have mercy offered, in the first place, to the biggest sinners.*

That these Jerusalem sinners were the biggest sinners that ever were in the world, I think none will deny, that believes that Christ was the best man that ever was in the world, and also was their Lord God. And that they were to have the first offer of his grace, the text is as clear as the sun; for it says, 'Beginning at Jerusalem.' 'Preach', says he, 'repentance and remission of sins' to the Jerusalem sinners: to the Jerusalem sinners in the *first* place. One would have thought, since the Jerusalem sinners were the worst and greatest sinners, Christ's greatest enemies, and those that not only despised his person, doctrine, and miracles, but that, a little before, had had their hands up to the elbows in his heart's blood, that he should rather have said, Go into all the world, and preach repentance and remission of sins among all nations; and, *after* that, offer the same to Jerusalem; yea, it had been infinite grace if he had said so. But what grace is this, or what name shall we give it, when he commands that this repentance and remission of sins, which is designed to be preached in all nations, should first be offered to Jerusalem; in the first place to the worst of sinners!

Nor was this the first time that the grace, which was in the heart of Christ, thus showed itself to the world. For while he was yet alive, even while he was yet in Jerusalem, and perceived, even among these Jerusalem sinners, those who were the most vile among them, he still, in his preaching did signify that he had a desire that the worst of these worst should, in the first place, come unto him. The which he showeth, where he says to the better sort of them, 'The publicans and the harlots go into the kingdom of God before you' (*Matt.* 21:31). Also when he compared Jerusalem with the sinners of the nations, then he commands that the Jerusalem sinners should have the gospel at present confined to them. 'Go not', says he, 'into the way of the Gentiles, and into *any* of the cities of the Samaritans enter ye not; but go rather to the lost sheep of the house of Israel' (*Matt.* 10:5–6; 23:37). But go rather to them, for they were in the most fearful plight. These, therefore, must have the cream of the gospel, namely, the first offer thereof, in his lifetime; yea, when he departed out of the world, he left this as part of his last will with his preachers, that they also should offer it first to Jerusalem. He had a mind, a careful mind, as it seems, to privilege the worst of sinners with the first offer of mercy, and to take from among them a people, to be the first fruits unto God and to the Lamb.

The 15th chapter of Luke also is famous for this, where the Lord Jesus takes more care, as appears there by three parables, for the lost sheep, the lost coin, and the prodigal son, than for the other sheep, the other coins, or for the son that said he had never transgressed; yea, he shows that there is joy in heaven, among the angels of God, at the repentance of one sinner, more than over ninety-nine just persons which need no repentance. After this manner, therefore, the mind of Christ was set on the salvation of the biggest sinners in his lifetime. But join to this, this clause, which he carefully put into the apostles' commission to preach, when he departed hence to the Father, and then you shall see that his heart was vehemently set upon it; for these were part of his last words with them, Preach my gospel to all nations, but see that you begin at Jerusalem.

Nor did the apostles overlook this clause when their Lord was gone into heaven; they went first to them of Jerusalem, and preached Christ's gospel to them; they abode also there for a season and time, and preached it to nobody else, for they had regard to the commandment of their Lord. And it is to be observed, namely, that the first sermon which they preached after the ascension of Christ, it was preached to the very worst of these Jerusalem sinners, even to those that were the murderers of Jesus Christ (*Acts* 2:23), for this is part of the sermon: 'Ye took him, and by wicked hands have crucified and slain him.' Yea, the next sermon, and the next, and also the next to that, was preached to the self-same murderers, to the end they might be saved (*Acts* 3:14–16; 4:10–11; 5:30; 7:52).

But we will return to the first sermon that was preached to these Jerusalem sinners, by which will be manifest more than great grace, if it be duly considered. For after Peter, and the rest of the apostles, had, in their exhortation, persuaded these wretches to believe that they had killed the Prince of life; and after they had duly fallen under the guilt of their murder, saying 'Men and brethren, what shall we do?', he replies by a universal tender to

[9]

them all in general, considering them as Christ's killers, that if they were sorry for what they had done, and would be baptized for the remission of their sins in his name, they should receive the gift of the Holy Ghost (*Acts* 2:37-38).

This he said to them all, though he knew that they were such sinners. Yea, he said it without the least stick or stop, or pause of spirit, as to whether he had best to say so or no. Nay, so far off was Peter from making an objection against one of them, that by a particular clause in his exhortation, he endeavours, that not one of them may escape the salvation offered. 'Repent,' says he, 'and be baptized every one of you.' I shut out not even one of you; for I am commanded by my Lord to deal with you, as it were, one by one, by the word of his salvation. But why speaks he so particularly? Oh! there were reasons for it. The people with whom the apostles were now to deal, as they were murderers of our Lord, and to be charged in general with his blood, so they had their various and particular acts of villainy in the guilt thereof now lying upon their consciences. And the guilt of these, their various and particular acts of wickedness, could not, perhaps, be reached to a removal thereof but by this particular application. Repent, every one of you; be baptized, every one of you, in his name, for the remission of sins, and you shall, every one of you, receive the gift of the Holy Ghost.

Objector: 'But I was one of them that plotted to take away his life. May I be saved by him?'

Peter: 'Every one of you.'

Objector: 'But I was one of them that bare false witness against him. Is there grace for me?'

Peter: 'For every one of you.'

Objector: 'But I was one of them that cried out, Crucify him, crucify him; and desired that Barabbas, the murderer, might live, rather than him. What will become of me, think you?'

Peter: 'I am to preach repentance and remission of sins to every one of you', says Peter.

Objector: 'But I was one of them that did spit in his face when he stood before his accusers. I also was one that mocked him, when in anguish he hung bleeding on the tree. Is there room for me?'

Peter: 'For every one of you', says Peter.

Objector: 'But I was one of them that, in his extremity, said, Give him gall and vinegar to drink. Why may not I expect the same when anguish and guilt is upon me?'

Peter: 'Repent of these your wickednesses, and here is remission of sins for every one of you.'

Objector: 'But I railed on him, I reviled him, I hated him, I rejoiced to see him mocked at by others. Can there be hopes for me?'

Peter: 'There is, for every one of you. Repent, and be baptized every one of you in the name of Jesus Christ, for the remission of sins, and ye shall receive the gift of the Holy Ghost.' Oh! what a blessed 'Every one of you' is here! How willing was Peter, and the Lord Jesus, by his ministry, to catch these murderers with the word of the gospel, that they might be made monuments of the grace of God! How unwilling, I say, was he, that any of these should escape the hand of mercy! Yea, what an amazing wonder is it to think that, above all the world, and above everybody in it, these should have the first offer of mercy! 'Beginning at Jerusalem.'

Was there not something of moment in this clause of the commission? Did not Peter, think you, see a great deal in it, that he should thus begin with these men, and thus offer, so particularly, this grace to each particular man of them?

But, as I told you, this is not all; these Jerusalem sinners must have this offer again and again; every one of them must be offered it over and over. Christ would not take their first rejection for a denial, nor their second repulse for a denial; but he will have grace offered once, and twice, and thrice, to these Jerusalem sinners. Is not this amazing grace? Christ will not be put off. These are the sinners that are sinners indeed. They are sinners of the biggest sort; consequently, such as Christ can, if they convert and be saved, best serve his ends and designs upon. Of which more later.

But what a pitch of grace is this! Christ is minded to amaze the world, and to show that he acts not like the children of men. This is that which he said of old, 'I will not execute the fierceness of my wrath, I will not return to destroy Ephraim; for I am God and not man' (*Hos.* 11:9, Geneva Bible). This is not the manner of men; men are shorter winded; men are soon moved to take vengeance, and to right themselves in a way of wrath and indignation. But God is full of grace, full of patience, ready to forgive, and one that delights in mercy. All this is seen in our text. The biggest sinners must first be offered mercy; they must, I say, have the cream of the gospel offered unto them.

But we will a little proceed. In the third chapter we find that they who escaped converting by the first sermon are called upon again to accept of grace and forgiveness, for their murder committed upon the Son of God. You have killed, yea, 'ye denied the Holy One and the Just, and desired a murderer to be granted unto you; and killed the Prince of life.' Mark, he falls again upon the very men that actually were, as you have it in the chapters following, his very betrayers and murderers (*Acts* 3:14–15); as being loth that they should escape the mercy of forgiveness: and exhorts them again to repent, that their sins might be 'blotted out' (verses 19–20).

Again, in the fourth chapter, he charges them afresh with this murder, (verse 10), but withal tells them salvation is in no other. Then, like a heavenly decoy, he puts himself also among them, to draw them the better under the net of the gospel; saying, 'There is none other name under heaven given among men, whereby we must be saved' (verse 12).

In the fifth chapter, you find them railing at him because he continued preaching among them salvation in the name of Jesus. But he tells them that that very Jesus whom they had slain and hanged on a tree, him God had raised up, and exalted 'to be a Prince and a Saviour, to give repentance to Israel, and forgiveness of sins' (verses

29–31). Still insinuating, that though they had killed him, and to this day rejected him, yet his business was to bestow upon them repentance and forgiveness of sins.

It is true that, after they began to kill again, and when nothing but killing would serve their turn, then they that were scattered abroad went everywhere preaching the Word. Yet even some of them so hankered after the conversion of the Jews, that they preached the gospel only to them. Also the apostles, still made their abode at Jerusalem, in hopes that they might let down their net for another draught of these Jerusalem sinners. Neither did Paul and Barnabas, who were the ministers of God to the Gentiles, but offer the gospel, in the first place, to those of them that, for their wickedness, were scattered, like vagabonds, among the nations; yea, and when they rendered rebellion and blasphemy for their service and love, they replied it was necessary that the Word of God should first have been spoken to them (*Acts* 1:8; 13:46–47).

Nor was this their preaching unsuccessful among these people: but the Lord Jesus so wrought with the Word thus spoken that thousands of them came flocking to him for mercy. Three thousand of them closed with him at the first; and, afterwards, two thousand more; for now they were in number about five thousand; whereas, before sermons were preached to these murderers, the number of the disciples was not above 'a hundred and twenty' (*Acts* 1:15; 2:41; 4:4).

Also, among these people that thus flocked to him for mercy there was a 'great company of the priests' (*Acts*

6:7). Now, the priests were they that were the greatest of these biggest sinners; they were the ringleaders, they were the inventors and ringleaders in the mischief. It was they that set the people against the Lord Jesus, and that were the cause why the uproar increased, until Pilate had given sentence upon him. 'The chief priests and elders', says the text, 'persuaded [the people] the multitude, that they should ask Barabbas, and destroy Jesus' (*Matt.* 27:20). And yet, behold, the priests, yea, a great company of the priests, became obedient to the faith.

Oh, the greatness of the grace of Christ, that he should be thus in love with the souls of Jerusalem sinners! that he should be thus delighted with the salvation of the Jerusalem sinners! that he should not only will that his gospel should be offered them, but that it should be offered unto them first, and before other sinners were admitted to a hearing of it. 'Begin at Jerusalem.'

Was this doctrine well believed, where would there be a place for a doubt or a fear of the damnation of the soul, if the sinner be penitent, how bad a life soever he has lived, how many soever in number are his sins? But this grace is hid from the eyes of men; the devil hides it from them; for he knows it is alluring, he knows it has an attracting virtue in it; for this is it that, above all arguments, can draw the soul to God. I cannot help it, but must let drop another word.

The first church, the Jerusalem church, from whence the gospel was to be sent into all the world, was a church made up of Jerusalem sinners. These great sinners were here the most shining monuments of the exceeding grace of God.

Thus, you see, I have proved the doctrine; and that not only by showing you that this was the practice of the Lord Jesus Christ in his lifetime, but his last will when he went up to God; saying, Begin to preach at Jerusalem. Yea, it is yet further manifested in that, when his ministers first began to preach there, he joined his power to the Word, to the converting of thousands of his betrayers and murderers, and also many of the ringleading priests, to the faith.

2

Why Mercy Is First Offered
to the Biggest Sinners

The observation, you know, is this: *Jesus Christ would have mercy offered, in the first place, to the biggest sinners, to the Jerusalem sinners*: 'Preach repentance, and remission of sins, in my name, among all nations, beginning at Jerusalem.'

The reasons of the point are:

FIRST, *Because the biggest sinners have most need thereof.*

He that has most need, reason says, should be helped first. I mean, when a helping hand is offered, and now it is; for the gospel of the grace of God is sent to help the world (*Acts* 16:9). But the biggest sinner has most need. Therefore, in reason, when mercy is sent down from heaven to men, the worst of men should have the first offer of it. 'Begin at Jerusalem.' This is the reason which the Lord Christ himself renders, why, in his lifetime, he left the best, and turned him to the worst; why he sat so loose from the righteous, and stuck so close to the wicked. 'The whole', saith he, 'have no need of the physician, but the sick. I came not to call the righteous, but the sinners to repentance' (*Mark* 2:15–17, Geneva Bible).

Above, you read that the scribes and Pharisees said to his disciples, 'How is it that he eateth and drinketh with publicans and sinners?' Alas! they did not know the reason; but the Lord renders them one, and such a one as is both natural and cogent, saying, These have need, most need. Their great necessity requires that I should be most friendly, and show my grace first to them.

Not that the other were sinless, and so had no need of a Saviour; but the publicans and their companions were the biggest sinners; they were, as to view, worse than the scribes; and, therefore, in reason, should be helped first, because they had most need of a Saviour.

Men that are at the point of death have more need of the physician than they that are only now and then troubled with a heart-fainting qualm. The publicans and sinners were, as it were, in the mouth of death; death was swallowing them down: and, therefore, the Lord Jesus receives them first; offers them mercy first. 'The whole have no need of the physician, but the sick. I came not to call the righteous, but the sinners to repentance.' The sick, as I said, is the biggest sinner, whether he sees his disease or not. He is stained from head to foot, from heart to life and conversation. This man, in every man's judgment, has the most need of mercy. There is nothing attends him from bed to board, and from board to bed again, but the visible characters, and obvious symptoms, of eternal damnation. This, therefore, is the man that has need, most need; and, therefore, in reason, should be helped in the first place. Thus it was with the people concerned in the text; they were the worst of sinners, Jerusalem sinners, sinners of the biggest size; and, therefore, such as had the greatest need; wherefore they must have mercy offered to them, before it be offered to anywhere else in the world. 'Begin at Jerusalem', offer mercy first to a Jerusalem sinner.

This man has most need, he is furthest from God, nearest to hell, and so one that has most need. This man's sins are in number the most, in cry the loudest, in weight the heaviest, and, consequently, will sink him soonest; wherefore he has most need of mercy. This man is shut up in Satan's hand, fastest bound in the cords of his sins: one that justice is whetting his sword to cut off; and, therefore, has most need, not only of mercy, but that it should be extended to him in the first place.

But a little further to show you the true nature of this reason, to wit, *That Jesus Christ would have mercy offered, in the first place, to the biggest sinners.*

First, mercy arises from the bowels and compassion, from pity, and from a feeling of the condition of those in misery. 'In his love, and in his pity, he redeemed them.' And again, 'The Lord is pitiful, very pitiful, and of tender mercy' (*Isa.* 63:9; *James* 5:11).

Now, where pity and compassion is, there is yearning of bowels; and where there is that, there is a readiness to help. And, I say again, the more deplorable and dreadful the condition is, the more directly do bowels and compassion turn themselves to such, and offer help and deliverance. All this flows from our first Scripture proof, I came to call them that have *need;* to call them first, while the rest look on and murmur.

'How shall I give thee up, Ephraim?' Ephraim was a revolter from God, a man that had given himself up to devilism; a company of men, the ten tribes that worshipped devils, while Judah kept with his God. But 'how shall I give thee up, Ephraim? *How* shall I deliver thee, Israel? *How* shall I make thee as Admah? How shall I set thee as Zeboim? (and yet thou art worse than they, nor has Samaria committed half thy sins, *Ezek.* 16:46–51) Mine heart is turned within me, my repentings are kindled together' (*Hos.* 11:8).

But where do you find that ever the Lord did thus rowl in his bowels[1] for and after any self-righteous man? No, no; they are the publicans and harlots, idolaters and Jerusalem sinners, for whom his bowels thus yearn and tumble about within him: for, alas! poor worms, they have most need of mercy.

Had not the good Samaritan more compassion for that man that fell among thieves (though that fall was occasioned by his going from the place where they worshipped God, to Jericho, the cursed city), than we read he had for any other besides? His wine was for him, his oil was for him, his beast for him; his penny, his care, and his

[1] Feel intense affection.

swaddling bands for him; for, alas! wretch, he had most need (*Luke*: 10:30–35).

Zaccheus the publican, the chief of the publicans, one that had made himself the richer by wronging of others; the Lord at that time singled him out from all the rest of his brother publicans, and that in the face of many Pharisees, and proclaimed in the audience of them all, that that day salvation was come to his house (*Luke* 19:1–8).

The woman, also, that had been bound down by Satan for eighteen years together, his compassions putting him upon it, he loosed her, though those that stood by snarled at him for so doing (*Luke* 13:11–13).

And why the woman of Sarepta, and why Naaman the Syrian, rather than widows and lepers of Israel, but because their conditions were more deplorable; for that they were most forlorn, and furthest from help (*Luke* 4:25, 27).

But I say, why all these, thus named? Why have we not a catalogue of some holy men that were so in their own eyes, and in the judgment of the world? Alas! if, at any time, any of them are mentioned, how seemingly coldly doth the record of Scripture present them to us? Nicodemus, a night professor, and Simon the Pharisee, with his fifty pence, and their great ignorance of the methods of grace, we have now and then touched upon.

Mercy seems to be out of its proper channel when it deals with self-righteous men; but then it rolls with a full stream when it extends itself to the biggest sinners. As God's mercy is not regulated by man's goodness, nor obtained by man's worthiness, so not much set out by saving of any such. But more of this later.

And here let me ask my reader a question: Suppose that, as you art walking by some pond side, you should see in it four or five children, all in danger of drowning, and one in more danger than all the rest; judge which has most need to be helped out first? I know you wilt say, he that is nearest drowning. Why, this is the case; the bigger sinner, the nearer drowning; therefore, the bigger sinner, the more need of mercy; yea, of help, by mercy, in the first place. And to this our text agrees, when it saith, 'Beginning at Jerusalem.' Let the Jerusalem sinner, says Christ, have the first offer, the first invitation, the first tender of my grace and mercy; for he is the biggest sinner, and so has most need thereof.

SECOND, Christ Jesus would have mercy offered, in the first place, to the biggest sinners, because *when they, any of them, receive it, it redounds most to the fame of his Name.*

Christ Jesus, as you may perceive, has put himself under the description of a physician, a doctor for curing of diseases; and you know that applause and fame are things that physicians much desire. That is what helps them to patients; and that, also, will help their patients to commit themselves to their skill, for cure, with the more confidence and repose of spirit. And the best way for a doctor or physician to get himself a name, is, in the first place, to take in hand, and cure, some such as all others have given up for lost and dead. Physicians get neither name nor fame by pricking of wheals,[1] or picking out thistles, or by laying of plasters to the scratch of a pin; every old woman can do this. But if they would have a name and a fame, if they will have it quickly, they must, as I said, do some great and desperate cures. Let them fetch one to life that was dead; let them recover one to his wits that was mad; let them make one that was born blind to see; or let them give ripe wits to a fool: these are notable cures, and he that can do thus, and if he doth thus first, he shall have the name and fame he desires; he may lie in bed till noon.

Why, Christ Jesus forgives sins for a name, and so begets for himself a good report in the hearts of the children of men. And, therefore, in reason he must be willing, as, also, he did command, that his mercy should be offered first to the biggest sinners. I will forgive their sins, iniquities, and transgressions, says he, 'And it shall be to me a name of joy, a praise and an honour, before all the nations of the earth' (*Jer.* 33:8–9). And hence it is that, at his first appearing, he took upon him to do such mighty works; he got a fame thereby, he got a name thereby (*Matt.* 4:23–24).

When Christ had cast the legion of devils out of the man of whom you read in Mark 5, he bade him go home to his friends, and tell it. 'Go home', saith he, 'to thy friends, and tell them how great things God hath done for thee, and hath had compassion on thee' (verse 19). Christ Jesus seeks a name, and desireth a fame in the world; and,

---

[1] Pustules or pimples

therefore, or the better to obtain that, he commands that mercy should first be proffered to the biggest sinners; because, by the saving of one of them, he makes all men marvel. As it is said of the man last mentioned, whom Christ cured towards the beginning of his ministry. 'And he departed,' says the text, 'and began to publish in Decapolis how great things Jesus had done for him; and all men did marvel' (*Mark* 5:20).

When John told Christ that they saw one casting out devils in his name, and they forbade him, because he followed not with them, what is the answer of Christ? 'Forbid him not; for there is no man which shall do a miracle in my name, that can lightly speak evil of me' (*Mark* 9:39). No; they will rather cause his praise to be heard, and his name to be magnified, and so put glory on the head of Christ.

But we will follow, a little, our metaphor. Christ, as I said, has put himself under the term of a physician; consequently, he desires that his fame, as to the salvation of sinners, may spread abroad, that the world may see what he can do. And to this end, he has not only commanded that the biggest sinners should have the first offer of his mercy, but has, as physicians do,[1] put out his bills, and published his doings, that things may be read and talked of. Yea, he has, moreover, in these, his blessed bills, the Holy Scriptures I mean, inserted the very names of persons, the places of their abode, and the great cures that, by the means of his salvation, he has wrought upon them

---

[1] In Bunyan's time, physicians regularly claimed wonderful cures.

[24]

to this very end. So we have, for example: such a one, by my grace and redeeming blood, was made a monument of everlasting life; and such a one, by my perfect obedience, became an heir of glory. And then he produces their names. I saved Lot from the guilt and damnation that he had procured for himself by his incest. I saved David from the vengeance that belonged to him for committing adultery and murder. Here is, also, Solomon, Manasseh, Peter, Magdalene, and many others, made mention of in this book. Here are their names, their sins, and their salvations recorded together, that you may read and know what a Saviour he is, and do him honour in the world. For why are these things thus recorded, but to show to sinners what he can do, to the praise and glory of his grace? And it is observable, as I said before, we have but very little of the salvation of *little* sinners mentioned in God's book, because that would not have answered the design, to wit, to bring glory and fame to the Name of the Son of God.

What should be the reason, think you, why Christ should so easily take a denial of the great ones that were the grandeur of the world, and struggle so hard for hedge-creepers[1] and highwaymen, as that parable seems to import he does, but to show forth the riches of the glory of his grace, to his praise (*Luke* 14)? This, I say, is one reason, to be sure. They that had their grounds, their yoke of oxen, and their marriage joys, were invited to come; but they made excuses, and that served the turn. But

[1] Stealthy rogues.

when he comes to deal with the worst, he says to his servants, Go out and bring them in hither. 'Go out quickly – and bring in hither the poor, the maimed, the halt, and the blind.' And they did so. And he said again, 'Go out into the highways and hedges, and compel them to come in, that my house may be filled' (*Luke* 14:18–19, 23). These poor, lame, maimed, blind, hedge-creepers, and highwaymen, must come in, must be forced in. These, if saved, will make his merit shine.

When Christ was crucified, and hanged up between the earth and heavens, there were two thieves crucified with him; and, behold, he lays hold of one of them, and will have him away with him to glory. Was not this a strange act, and a display of unthought-of grace? Were there none but thieves there, or were the rest of that company out of his reach? Could he not, think you, have stooped from the cross to the ground, and have laid hold on some more honest man, if he would? Yes, doubtless. Oh! but then he would not have displayed his grace, nor so have pursued his own designs, namely, to get to himself a praise and a name; but now he has done it deliberately. For who that shall read this story but must confess that the Son of God is full of grace; for a proof of the riches thereof he left behind him, when, upon the cross, he took the thief away with him to glory.

Nor can this one act of his be buried; it will be talked of, to the end of the world, to his praise. '*Men* shall speak of the might of thy terrible acts, and I will declare thy greatness. They shall abundantly utter the memory of thy great goodness, and shall sing of thy righteousness. They shall speak of the glory of thy kingdom, and talk of thy power; to make known to the sons of men his mighty acts, and the glorious majesty of his kingdom' (*Psa.* 145:6–12).

When the Word of God came among the conjurors and those soothsayers that you read of in Acts 19, and had prevailed with some of them to accept the grace of Christ, the Holy Ghost records it with a boast, for that it would redound to his praise, saying, 'Many of them also which used curious arts brought their books together, and burned them before all men; and they counted the price of them, and found it fifty thousand pieces of silver. So mightily grew the Word of God, and prevailed' (*Acts* 19:19–20). It wrenched out of the clutches of Satan some of those of whom he thought himself most sure. 'So mightily grew the Word of God.' It grew mightily, it encroached upon the kingdom of the devil. It pursued him, and took the prey; it forced him to let go his hold! It brought away captive, as prisoners taken by force of arms, some of the most valiant of his army. It fetched back from, as it were, the confines of hell, some of those that were his most trusty, and that, with hell, had been at an agreement. It made them come and confess their deeds, and burn their books before all men. 'So mightily grew the Word of God, and prevailed.'

Thus, therefore, you see why Christ will have offered mercy, in the first place, to the biggest sinners; they have most need thereof; and this is the most ready way to extol his name 'that rideth upon the heavens' to our help.

THIRD, Christ Jesus would have mercy offered, in the first place, to the biggest sinners, because, *by their forgiveness and salvation, others, hearing of it, will be encouraged the more to come to him for life.*

For the physician, by curing the most desperate at the first, does not only get himself a name but begets encouragement in the minds of other diseased folk to come to him for help. Hence you read of our Lord that, when, through his tender mercy, he had cured many of great diseases, his fame was spread abroad: 'They brought unto him all sick people that were taken with divers diseases and torments, and those which were possessed with devils, and those which were lunatic, and those that had the palsy, and he healed them. And there followed him great multitudes of people from Galilee, and Decapolis, and Jerusalem, and Judea, and from beyond Jordan' (*Matt.* 4:24–25). See here, he first, by working, gets himself a fame, a name, and renown; and now men take encouragement, and bring, from all quarters, their diseased to him, being helped, by what they had heard, to believe that their diseased should be healed.

Now, as he did with those outward cures, so he does in the proffers of his grace and mercy; he proffers it, in the first place, to the biggest sinners, that others may take heart to come to him to be saved. I will give you a Scripture or two to show you that Christ, by commanding that his mercy should, in the first place, be offered to the biggest of sinners, has a design thereby to encourage and provoke others to come also to him for mercy. 'God,' says Paul, 'who is rich in mercy, for his great love wherewith he loved us, even when we were dead in sins, hath quickened us together with Christ (by grace ye are saved); and hath raised us up together, and made us sit together in heavenly places in Christ Jesus.' But why did he do all this? 'That in the ages to come he might show the exceeding riches of his grace in his kindness towards us through Christ Jesus' (*Eph.* 2:4–7). See, here is a design; God lets out his mercy to Ephesus of design, even to show to the ages to come the exceeding riches of his grace, in his kindness to them through Christ Jesus. And why to show, by these, the exceeding riches of his grace to the ages to come through Christ Jesus? Why but to allure them and their children also to come to him, and to partake of the same grace through Christ Jesus?

But what was Paul, and the Ephesian sinners (of Paul we will speak later)? These Ephesian sinners were men dead in sins; men that walked according to the dictates and motions of the devil; worshippers of Diana, that effeminate goddess; men far off from God, aliens and strangers to all good things; such as were far off from these, as I said, and, consequently, in a most deplorable condition. As the Jerusalem sinners were of the highest sort among the Jews, so these Ephesian sinners were of the highest sort among the Gentiles (*Eph.* 2:1–3, 11–12; *Acts* 19:35). Wherefore, as by the Jerusalem sinners, in saving them first, he had a design to provoke others to come to him for mercy, so the same design is here set on foot again, in his calling and converting the Ephesian sinners:

'That in the ages to come he might show the exceeding riches of his grace', says he, 'in his kindness towards us through Christ Jesus.' There is yet one hint more. It is said that God saved these 'for his great love'; that is, as I think, for the setting forth, for the commendation of his love, for the advance of his love, in the hearts and minds of them that should come after. As if he should say, God has had mercy upon and been gracious to you, that he might show to others, for their encouragement, that they have ground to come to him to be saved. When God saves one great sinner, it is to encourage another great sinner to come to him for mercy.

He saved the thief to encourage thieves to come to him for mercy; he saved Magdalene to encourage other Magdalenes to come to him for mercy; he saved Saul to encourage Sauls to come to him for mercy; and this Paul himself doth say, 'For this cause', saith he, 'I obtained mercy, that in me first Jesus Christ might show forth all long-suffering, for a pattern to them which should hereafter believe on him to life everlasting' (*1 Tim.* 1:16). How plain are the words! Christ, in saving me, has given to the world a pattern of his grace, that they might see, and believe, and come, and be saved; that they that are to be born hereafter might believe on Jesus Christ to life everlasting.

But what was Paul? Why, he tells you himself; I am, says he, the chief of sinners. I was, says he, a blasphemer, a persecutor, an injurious person; but I obtained mercy (*1 Tim.* 1:13–14). Aye, that is well for you, Paul; but what advantage have we thereby? Oh, very much, says he; for, 'for this cause I obtained mercy, that in me first Jesus Christ might show forth all longsuffering, for a pattern to them which should hereafter believe on him to life everlasting' (verse 16). Thus, therefore, you see that this third reason is of strength; namely, that Jesus Christ would have mercy offered, in the first place, to the biggest sinners, because, by their forgiveness and salvation, others, hearing of it, will be encouraged the more to come to him for mercy. It may well, therefore, be said to God, Thou delightest in mercy, and mercy pleases thee (*Mic.* 7:18).

But who believes that this was God's design in showing mercy of old, namely, that we that come after might take courage to come to him for mercy; or that Jesus Christ would have mercy offered, in the first place, to the biggest sinners to stir up others to come to him for life? This is not the manner of men, O God! But David saw this quickly; therefore he makes this one argument with God, that he would blot out his transgressions, that he would forgive his adultery, his murders, and horrible hypocrisy. Do it, O Lord, saith he, do it, and 'then will I teach transgressors thy ways, and sinners shall be converted unto thee' (*Psa.* 51:7–13). He knew that the conversion of sinners would be a work highly pleasing to God, as being that which he had designed before he made mountain or hill: wherefore he comes, and he says, Save me, O Lord; if thou wilt but save me, I will fall in with thy design; I will help to bring what sinners to thee I can. And, Lord, I am willing to be made a preacher myself, for that I have been a horrible sinner; wherefore, if thou shalt forgive my great transgressions, I shall be a fit man to tell of thy wondrous grace to others. Yea, Lord, I dare promise that, if thou wilt have mercy upon me, it shall tend to the glory of thy grace, and also to the increase of thy kingdom; for I will tell it, and sinners will hear about it. And there is nothing so suited to the hearing sinner as mercy, and to be informed that God is willing to bestow it upon him. 'I will teach transgressors thy ways; and sinners shall be converted unto thee.'

Nor will Christ Jesus miss of his design in proffering mercy, in the first place, to the biggest sinners. You know what work the Lord, by laying hold of the woman of Samaria, made among the people there. They knew that she was a town sinner, an adulteress; yea, one that, after the most audacious manner, lived in uncleanness with a man that was not her husband. But when she, from a turn upon her heart, went into the city, and said to her neighbours, 'Come', Oh, how they came! how they flocked out of the city to Jesus Christ! 'Then they went out of the city, and came to him.' 'And many of the Samaritans of that city [people, perhaps, as bad as herself] believed on him for the saying of the woman, which testified, He told me all that ever I did' (*John* 4:39). That word, 'He told me all that ever I did', was a great argument with them; for by that they gathered that, though he knew her to be vile, yet he did not despise her, nor refuse to show how willing he was to communicate his grace unto her; and this fetched over, first her, then them.

This woman, as I said, was a Samaritan sinner, a sinner of the worst complexion; for the Jews abhorred to have anything to do with them (verse 9), wherefore none more fit than she to be made one of the decoys of heaven, to bring others of these Samaritan wild-fowls under the net of the grace of Christ; and she did the work well. Many and many more of the Samaritans believed on him (verses 40–42). The heart of man, though set on sin, will, when it comes once to a persuasion that God is willing to have mercy upon us, incline to come to Jesus Christ for life. Witness those turn-aways from God that you also read of in Jeremiah; for after they had heard, three or four times over, that God had mercy for backsliders, they broke out and said, 'Behold, we come unto thee; for thou art the LORD our God' (*Jer.* 3:22); or, as those in Hosea said, 'For in thee the fatherless findeth mercy' (*Hos.* 14:1–3).

Mercy, and the revelation thereof, is the only antidote against sin. It is of a thawing nature; it will loose the heart that is frozen up in sin; yea, it will make the unwilling willing to come to Jesus Christ for life. Why do you think it was that Jesus Christ told the adulterous woman, and that before so many sinners, that he had not condemned her, but to allure her, with them there present, to hope to find favour at his hands? As he also saith, in another place, 'I came not to judge, but to save the world.' For

[33]

might they not thence most rationally conclude that, if Jesus Christ would rather save than damn a harlot, there was encouragement for them (although great sinners) to come to him for mercy?

I once heard a story from a soldier who, with his company, had laid siege against a fort, that so long as the besieged were persuaded their foes would show them no favour, they fought like madmen; but when they saw one of their fellows taken, and received to favour, they all came tumbling down from their fortress, and delivered themselves into their enemies' hands. I am persuaded, did men believe that there is that grace and willingness in the heart of Christ to save sinners, as the Word imports there is, they would come tumbling into his arms: but Satan has blinded their minds so that they cannot see this thing. However, the Lord Jesus has, as I said, so that others might take heart and come to him, given out a commandment, that mercy should, in the first place, be offered to the biggest sinners. 'Begin', saith he, 'at Jerusalem'; and thus I end the third reason.

FOURTH, Jesus Christ would have mercy offered, in the first place, to the biggest sinners, because *that is the way, if they receive it, most to weaken the kingdom of Satan, and to keep it lowest in every age of the world.*

The biggest sinners, they are Satan's colonels and captains, the leaders of his people, and they that most stoutly make head against the Son of God. Wherefore, let these first be conquered, and his kingdom will be weak.

When Ishbosheth had lost his Abner, the kingdom was made weak, nor did he sit but tottering then upon his throne. So, when Satan loses his strong men, them that are mighty to work iniquity, and dexterous to manage others in the same, then is his kingdom weak (2 *Sam.* 3). Therefore, I say, Christ does offer mercy in the first place to such, the more to weaken his kingdom. Christ Jesus was glad to see Satan fall like lightning from heaven; that is, suddenly, or headlong; and it was, surely, by casting of him out of strong possession, and by recovering of some notorious sinners out of his clutches (*Luke* 10:17–19).

Samson, when he would pull down the Philistines' temple, took hold of the two main pillars of it, and, breaking them, down came the house. Christ came to destroy the works of the devil, and to destroy by converting grace, as well as by redeeming blood. Now, sin swarms, and flesh lies by legions and whole armies, in the souls of the biggest sinners, as in garrisons; wherefore, the way, the most direct way, to destroy it is first to deal with such sinners by the word of his gospel, and by the merits of his passion.

For example, though I shall give you but a homely one, suppose a family to be very louse-infested, and one or two of the family to be the chief breeders, the way, the quickest way, to clear that family, or at least to weaken the swarming of those vermin, is, in the first place, to sweeten the skin, head, and clothes of the chief breeders; and then, though all the family should be apt to breed them, the number of them, and so the greatness of that plague there, will be the more impaired. Why, there are some people that are the devil's chief sin-breeders in the towns and places where they live. The place, town, or family where they live must needs be horribly lousy, and, as it were, eaten up with vermin. Now, let the Lord Jesus, in the first place, cleanse these great breeders, and there will be given a nip to those swarms of sins that used to be committed in such places throughout the town, house, or family, where such sin-breeding persons used to be.

I speak by experience. I was one of these lousy ones, one of these great sin-breeders; I infected all the youth of the town where I was born, with all manner of youthful vanities. The neighbours counted me so; my practice proved me so: wherefore Christ Jesus took me first; and taking me first, the contagion was much allayed all the town over. When God made me sigh, they would hearken, and inquiringly say, What's the matter with John? They also gave their various opinions of me; but, as I said, sin cooled, and failed, as to his full career. When I went out to seek the bread of life, some of them would follow, and the rest were put into a muse[1] at home. Yea, almost the town, at first, at times would go out to hear at the place where I found good; yea, young and old for a while had some reformation on them; also some of them, perceiving that God had mercy upon me, came crying to him for mercy too.

But what need I give you an instance of poor I; I will come to Manasseh the king. So long as he was a

---

[1] Made to think deeply.

ringleading sinner, the great idolater, and chief for devilism, the whole land flowed with wickedness; for he made them to sin (2 *Chron.* 33) and do worse than the heathen that dwelt round about them, or that was cast out from before them: but when God converted him, the whole land was reformed. Down went the groves, the idols, and altars of Baal, and up went true religion in much of the power and purity of it. You will say, the king reformed by power. I answer, doubtless, and by example too; for people observe their leaders; as their fathers did, so did they (2 *Kings* 17:41). This, therefore, is another reason why Jesus would have mercy offered, in the first place, to the biggest sinners, because that is the best way, if they receive it, most to weaken the kingdom of Satan, and to keep it poor and low.

And do you not think now that if God would but take hold of the hearts of some of the most notorious in your town, in your family, or country, that this thing would be verified before your faces? It would, it would, to the joy of you that are godly, to the making of hell to sigh, to the great suppressing of sin, the glory of Christ, and the joy of the angels of God. And ministers should, therefore, that this work might go on, take advantages to persuade the biggest sinners to come in to Christ, according to my text, and their commission, 'Beginning at Jerusalem.'

FIFTH, Jesus Christ would have mercy offered, in the first place, to the biggest sinners, because *such, when converted, are usually the best helps in the church against temptations, and fittest for the support of the feeble-minded there.*

Hence, usually, you have some such in the first plantation of churches, or quickly upon it. Churches would do but sorrily if Christ Jesus did not put such converts among them; they are the monuments and mirrors of mercy. The very sight of such a sinner in God's house, yea, the very thought of him, where the sight of him cannot be had, is ofttimes greatly for the help of the faith of the feeble.

When the churches, says Paul, that were in Judea, heard this concerning me, that he which persecuted them in time past, now preached the faith which once he destroyed, 'they glorified God in me' (*Gal.* 1:20–24). 'Glorified God'? How is that? Why, they praised him, and took courage to believe the more in the mercy of God; for that he had had mercy on such a great sinner as he. They glorified God 'in me'; they wondered that grace should be so rich as to take hold of such a wretch as I was; and for my sake believed in Christ the more.

There are two things that great sinners are acquainted with which, when they come to divulge them to the saints, are a great relief to their faith. 1. *The contests that they usually have with the devil* at their parting with him. 2. *Their knowledge of his secrets* in his workings.

1. For first, *the biggest sinners have usually great contests with the devil at their partings;* and this is an help to saints: for ordinary saints find afterwards what the vile ones find at first, but when, at the opening of hearts, the

one finds himself to be as the other – the one is a comfort
to the other. The lesser sort of sinners find but little of this
till after they have been some time in profession; but the
vile man meets with this at the beginning. Wherefore he,
when the other is down, is ready to tell that he has met
with the same before; for, I say, he has had it before.
Satan is loth to part with a great sinner. 'What, my true
servant,' says he, 'my old servant, will you forsake me
now? Having so often sold yourself to me to work wickedness, will you forsake me now? You horrible wretch, do
you not know that you have sinned yourself beyond the
reach of grace, and do you think to find mercy now? Are
you not a murderer, a thief, a harlot, a witch, a sinner of
the greatest size, and do you look for mercy now? Do you
think that Christ will foul his fingers with you? It is
enough to make angels blush, says Satan, to see so vile a
one knock at heaven-gates for mercy, and will you be so
abominably bold as to do it?'

Thus Satan dealt with me, says the great sinner, when at
first I came to Jesus Christ. And what did you reply? says
the tempted. Why, I granted the whole charge to be true,
says the other. And what, did you despair, or how? No,
saith he, I said, I am Magdalene, I am Zaccheus, I am the
thief, I am the harlot, I am the publican, I am the prodigal, and one of Christ's murderers; yea, worse than any of
these; and yet God was so far off from rejecting me, as I
found afterwards, that there was music and dancing in his
house for me, and for joy that I was come home to him.
O blessed be God for grace (says the other), for then I

hope, there is favour for me. Yea, as I told you, such a one is a continual spectacle in the church for every one to behold God's grace and wonder at.

2. And as for *the secrets of Satan,* such as are suggestions to question the being of God, the truth of his Word, and to be annoyed with devilish blasphemies; none are more acquainted with these than the biggest sinners at their conversion; wherefore thus also they are prepared to be helps in the church to relieve and comfort the other.

I might also here tell you of the contests and battles that such are engaged in, wherein they find the buffetings of Satan above any other of the saints. At which time Satan assaults the soul with darkness, fears, frightful thoughts, and apparitions; now they sweat, pant, cry out, and struggle for life. The angels now come down to behold the sight, and rejoice to see a bit of dust and ashes overcome principalities and powers, and might, and dominions. But, as I said, when these come to be a little settled, they are prepared for helps for others, and are great comforts unto them. Their great sins give encouragement to the devil to assault them; and by these temptations Christ takes advantage to make them the more helpful to the churches.

The biggest sinner, when he is converted and comes into the church, says to them all, by his very coming in, Behold me, all you that are men and women of a low and timorous spirit, you whose hearts are narrow, for that you never had the advantage to know, because your sins are few, the largeness of the grace of God. Behold, I say, in me, the exceeding riches of his grace! I am a pattern set forth before your faces, on whom you may look and take heart. This, I say, the great sinner can say, to the exceeding comfort of all the rest. Wherefore, as I have hinted before, when God intends to stock a place with saints, and make that place excellently to flourish with the riches of his grace, he usually begins with the conversion of some of the most notorious thereabouts and lays them as an example to allure others, and to build up when they are converted. It was Paul that must go to the Gentiles because Paul was the most outrageous of all the apostles in the time of his unregeneracy. Yea, Peter must be he that, after his horrible fall, was thought fittest, when recovered again, to comfort and strength his brethren (see *Luke* 22:31–32).

Some must be pillars in God's house; and if they be pillars of cedar, so they must stand while they are stout and sturdy sticks in the forest, before they are cut down, and planted or placed there. No man, when he builds his house, makes the principal parts thereof of weak or feeble timber – for how could such bear up the rest? – but of great and able wood. Christ Jesus also goes this way to work; he makes of the biggest sinners bearers and supporters to the rest. This, then, may serve for another reason why Jesus Christ gives out in commandment that mercy should, in the first place, be offered to the biggest sinners, because such, when converted, are usually the best helps in the church against temptations, and fittest for the support of the feeble-minded there.

SIXTH, Another reason why Jesus Christ would have mercy offered, in the first place, to the biggest sinners is because *they, when converted, are apt to love him most.*

This agrees both with Scripture and reason. Scripture says so. To whom much is forgiven, the same loves much. 'To whom little is forgiven, the same loveth little' (*Luke* 7:47). Reason says so: for as it would be the most unreasonable thing in the world to render hatred for love, and contempt for forgiveness; so it would be as ridiculous to think that the reception of a little kindness should lay the same obligations upon the heart to love as the reception of a great deal. I would not disparage the love of Christ; I know the minutest weight of it, when it reaches to forgiveness, is great above all the world; but comparatively there are greater extensions of the love of Christ to one than to another. He that has most sin, if forgiven, is partaker of the greatest love, of the greatest forgiveness.

I know also, that there are some that, from this very doctrine, say, 'Let us do evil that good may come'; and that turn the grace of our God into lasciviousness. But I speak not of these; these will neither be ruled by grace nor reason. Grace would teach them, if they knew it, to deny ungodly courses; and so would reason too, if it could truly sense the love of God (*Titus* 2:11–12; *Rom.* 12:1).

Does it look like what has any coherence with reason or mercy for a man to abuse his friend? Because Christ died for men, shall I therefore spit in his face? The bread and water that was given by Elisha to his enemies that came into the land of Israel to take him had so much influence upon their minds, though heathens, that they returned to their homes without hurting him; yea, it kept them from coming again in a hostile manner into the coasts of Israel (2 *Kings* 6:19–23).

But I forbear to illustrate till later. One reason why Christ Jesus shows mercy to sinners is that he might obtain their love, that he may remove their base affections from base objects to himself. Now, if he loves to be loved a little, he loves to be loved much; but there is not any that are capable of loving much, save those that have much forgiven them.

Hence it is said of Paul that he laboured more than them all; to wit, with a labour of love, because he had been by sin more vile against Christ than they all (*1 Cor.* 15). He it was that 'persecuted the church of God, and wasted it' (*Gal.* 1:13). He of them all was the only raving maniac against the saints. 'And being exceeding mad', says he, 'against them, I persecuted them even unto strange cities' (*Acts* 26:11). This raving maniac, that once was so, is he that now says, I laboured more than them all, more for Christ than them all. But Paul, what moved you thus to do? The love of Christ, says he. It was not I, but the grace of God that was with me. As if to say, O grace! It was such grace to save me! It was such marvellous grace for God to look down from heaven upon me, and that secured me from the wrath to come, that I am captivated with the sense of the riches of it. Hence I act, hence I labour; for how can I otherwise do, since God not only separated me from my sins and companions, but

separated all the powers of my soul and body to his service? I am, therefore, prompted on by this exceeding love
to labour as I have done; yet not I, but the grace of God
with me. Oh! I shall never forget his love, nor the circumstances under which I was, when his love laid hold upon
me. I was going to Damascus with letters from the high-
priest, to make havoc of God's people there, as I had
made havoc of them in other places. These bloody letters
were not imposed upon me. I went to the high-priest and
desired them of him, and yet he saved me (*Acts* 9:1–2)! I
was one of the men, of the chief men, that had a hand in
the blood of his martyr Stephen; yet he had mercy upon
me! When I was at Damascus, I stuck so horribly, like a
blood-sucker, that I became a terror to all thereabout.
Yea, Ananias, a good man, made intercession to my Lord
against me; yet he would have mercy upon me, yea,
joined mercy to mercy, until he had made me a monument
of grace. He made a saint of me, and persuaded me that
my transgressions were forgiven me.

When I began to preach, those that heard me were
amazed, and said, 'Is not this he that destroyed them that
called on this name in Jerusalem, and came hither for that
intent, that he might bring them bound to the high-
priest?' Hell doth know that I was a sinner; heaven doth
know that I was a sinner; the world also knows that I was
a sinner, a sinner of the greatest size; but I obtained mercy
(*Acts* 9:20–21). Shall not this lay obligation upon me? Is
not love of the greatest force to oblige? Is it not strong as
death, cruel as the grave, and hotter than the coals of

juniper? Hath it not a most vehement flame? Can the waters quench it? Can the floods drown it? I am under the force of it, and this is my continual cry, What shall I render to the Lord for all the benefits which he has bestowed upon me?

Aye, Paul! this is something; you speak like a man, like a man affected, and carried away with the love and grace of God. Now this sense, and this affection, and this labour, gives to Christ the love that he looks for. But he might have converted twenty little sinners, and yet not found, for grace bestowed, so much love in them all. I wonder how far a man might go among the converted sinners of the smaller size before he could find one that so much as looked anything like this. Where is he that is thus under pangs of love for the grace bestowed upon him by Jesus Christ? Excepting only some few, you may walk to the world's end, and find none. But, as I said, some there are, and so there have been in every age of the church, great sinners that have had much forgiven them; and they love much upon this account. Jesus Christ, therefore, knows what he is doing when he lays hold on the hearts of sinners of the biggest size. He knows that such a one will love more than many that have not sinned half their sins.

I will tell you a story that I have read of Martha and Mary. The name of the book I have forgotten, I mean of the book in which I found the relation; but the thing was thus: Martha, said my author, was a very holy woman, much like Lazarus, her brother; but Mary was a loose and wanton creature; Martha did seldom miss good sermons and lectures, when she could come at them in Jerusalem; but Mary would frequent the house of sports, and the company of the vilest of men for lust. And though Martha had often desired that her sister would go with her to hear her preachers, yea, had often entreated her with tears to do it, yet could she never prevail; for still Mary would make her excuse, or reject her with disdain, for her zeal and preciseness in religion.

After Martha had waited long and tried many ways to bring her sister to good, and all had proved ineffectual, at last she comes upon her thus: 'Sister,' says she, 'I pray you, go with me to the temple today to hear one preach a sermon.' 'What kind of preacher is he?' said she. Martha replied, 'It is one Jesus of Nazareth; he is the handsomest man that ever you saw with your eyes. Oh! he shines in beauty, and is a most excellent preacher.'

Now, what does Mary, after a little pause, but goes up into her chamber, and, with her pins and her clouts,[1] decks up herself as fine as her fingers could make her. This done, away she goes, not with her sister Martha, but as much unobserved as she could, to the sermon, or rather to see the preacher.

The hour and preacher being come, and she having observed whereabout the preacher would stand, goes and sets herself so in the temple that she might be sure to have the full view of this excellent person. So he comes in, and she looks, and the first glimpse of his person pleases her.

[1] Pieces of cloth.

Well, Jesus addresses himself to his sermon, and she looks earnestly on him.

Now, at that time, says my author, Jesus preached about the lost sheep, the lost coin, and the prodigal son. And when he came to show what care the shepherd took for one lost sheep, and how the woman swept to find her piece which was lost, and what joy there was at their finding, she began to be taken by the ears, and forgot what she came about, musing what the preacher would make of it. But when he came to the application, and showed, that by the lost sheep, was meant a great sinner; by the shepherd's care, was meant God's love for great sinners; and that by the joy of the neighbours was showed what joy there was among the angels in heaven over one great sinner that repents, she began to be taken by the heart. And as he spoke these last words, she thought he pitched his innocent eyes just upon her, and looked as if he spoke what was now said to *her*: wherefore her heart began to tremble, being shaken with affection and fear; then her eyes ran down with tears apace; wherefore she was forced to hide her face with her handkerchief, and so sat sobbing and crying all the rest of the sermon.

Sermon being done, up she gets, and away she goes, and withal inquired where this Jesus the preacher dined that day? And one told her, At the house of Simon the Pharisee. So away goes she, first to her chamber, and there strips herself of her wanton attire; then falls upon her knees to ask God forgiveness for all her wicked life. This done, in a modest dress she goes to Simon's house where she finds Jesus sat at dinner. So she gets behind him, and weeps, and drops her tears upon his feet like rain, and washes them, and wipes them with the hair of her head. She also kisses his feet with her lips, and anoints them with ointment.

When Simon the Pharisee perceived what the woman did, and being ignorant of what it was to be forgiven much (for he never was forgiven more than fifty pence), he began to think within himself, that he had been mistaken about Jesus Christ, because he suffered such a sinner as this woman was, to touch him. Surely, said he, this man, if he were a prophet, would not let this woman come near him, for she is a town-sinner; so ignorant are all self-righteous men of the way of Christ with sinners.

But, lest Mary should be discouraged with some clownish carriage of this Pharisee, and so desert her good beginnings, and her new steps which she now had begun to take towards eternal life, Jesus began thus with Simon: 'Simon,' said he, 'I have somewhat to say unto thee.' And he saith, 'Master, say on.' 'There was', said Jesus, 'a certain creditor which had two debtors; the one owed five hundred pence, and the other fifty. And when they had nothing to pay, he frankly forgave them both. Tell me, therefore, which of them will love him most? Simon answered, and said, I suppose that he, to whom he forgave most. And he said unto him, Thou hast rightly judged. And he turned to the woman, and said unto Simon, Seest thou this woman? I entered into thine house, thou gavest me no water for my feet; but she hath washed my feet with tears, and wiped them with the hairs of her head. Thou gavest me no kiss; but this woman, since the time I came in, hath not ceased to kiss my feet. My head with oil thou didst not anoint, but this woman hath anointed my feet with ointment. Wherefore, I say unto her, Her sins, which are many, are forgiven, for she loved much; but to whom little is forgiven, the same loveth little. And he said unto her, Thy sins are forgiven' (*Luke* 7:36–18).

Thus you have the story. If I come short in any circumstance, I beg pardon of those that can correct me. It is twenty-three or four years since I saw the book; yet I have, as far as my memory will admit, given you the relation of the matter. However, Luke, as you see, doth here present you with the substance of the whole.[1]

Alas! Christ Jesus has but little thanks for the saving of little sinners. 'To whom little is forgiven, the same loveth little.' He gets not water for his feet, by his saving of such sinners.

There are abundance of dry-eyed Christians in the world, and abundance of dry-eyed duties too; duties that never were wetted with the tears of contrition and repentance, nor ever sweetened with the great sinner's box of ointment. And the reason is, such sinners have not great sins to be saved from; or, if they have, they look upon them in the diminishing glass[2] of the holy law of God.

---

[1] It was a commonly received opinion among ancient writers that Mary Magdalene was the sister of Martha and Lazarus.
[2] A lens or combination of lenses that makes objects look smaller.

[49]

But I rather believe that the professors of our days lack a due sense of what they are; for, truly, for the generality of them, both before and since conversion, they have been sinners of a lusty size. But if their eyes be holden, if convictions are not shown, if their knowledge of their sins is but like the eyesight in twilight, the heart cannot be affected with that grace that has laid hold on the man; and so Christ Jesus sows much, and has little coming in. Wherefore his way is oftentimes to step out of the way, to Jericho, to Samaria, to the country of the Gadarenes, to the coasts of Tyre and Sidon, and also to Mount Calvary, that he may lay hold of such kind of sinners as will love him to his liking (*Luke* 19:1-11; *John* 4:3-11; *Mark* 5:1-20; *Matt.* 15:21-29; *Luke* 23:33-43).

But thus much for the sixth reason, why Christ Jesus would have mercy offered, in the first place, to the biggest sinners, to wit, because such sinners, when converted, are apt to love him most. The Jerusalem sinners were they that outstripped, when they were converted, in some things, all the churches of the Gentiles. They were 'of one heart and of one soul: neither said any of them that ought of the things which he possessed was his own . . . Neither was there any among them that lacked: for as many as were possessors of lands or houses sold them, and brought the prices of the things that were sold, and laid them down at the apostles' feet', etc. (*Acts* 4:32, 35). Now, show me such another pattern, if you can. But why did these do thus? Oh! they were Jerusalem sinners. These were the men that, but a little before, had killed the Prince of life; and those to whom he did, that notwithstanding, send the first offer of grace and mercy. And the sense of this took them up between the earth and the heaven, and carried them on in such ways and methods as could never be trodden by any since. They talk of the church of Rome and set her, in her primitive state, as a pattern and mother of churches, when the truth is, it was the Jerusalem sinners, when converts, that outdid all the churches that ever were.

SEVENTH, Christ Jesus would have mercy offered, in the first place, to the biggest sinners, because *grace, when it is received by such, finds matter to kindle upon more freely than it finds in other sinners.*

Great sinners are like the dry wood, or like great candles, which burn best and shine with the biggest light. I lay not this down, as I did those reasons before, to show that when great sinners are converted they will be encouragement to others, though that is true; but to show, that Christ has a delight to see grace, the grace we receive, to shine. We love to see things that bear a good gloss; yea, we choose to buy such kind of matter to work upon as will, if wrought up to what we intend, cast that lustre that we desire. Candles that burn not brightly we like not; wood that is green will rather smother, and sputter, and smoke, and crack, and flounce, than cast a brave light and a pleasant heat; wherefore great folks care not much, not so much, for such kind of things as for them that will better answer their ends.

Hence Christ desires the biggest sinner; in him there is matter to work with, to wit, a great deal of sin; for as by the tallow of the candle the fire takes occasion to burn the brighter, so, by the sin of the soul grace takes occasion to shine the clearer. Little candles shine but little, for there is a want of matter for the fire to work on; but in the great sinner, there is more matter for grace to work on. Faith shines when it works towards Christ through the sides of many and great transgressions, and so does love, because much is forgiven. And what matter can be found in the soul for humility to work by so well as by a sight that I have been and am an abominable sinner? And the same is to be said of patience, meekness, gentleness, self-denial, or of any other grace.

Grace takes occasion, by the vileness of the man, to shine the more; even as by the ruggedness of a very strong distemper or disease, the virtue of the medicine is best made manifest. 'Where sin abounded, grace did much more abound' (*Rom.* 5:20). A black string makes the neck look whiter; great sins make grace burn clearly. Some say that when grace and a good nature meet together, they do make shining Christians; but I say, when grace and a great sinner meet, and when grace shall subdue that great sinner to itself, and shall operate after its kind in the soul of that great sinner, *then* we have a shining Christian; witness all those of whom mention was made before.

Abraham was among the idolaters when in the land of Assyria, and served idols, with his kindred, on the other side of the River (*Josh.* 24:2; *Gen.* 11:31). But who, when called, was there in the world in whom grace shone so bright as in him? The Thessalonians were idolaters before the Word of God came to them; but when they had received it, they became examples to all that did believe in Macedonia and Achaia (*1 Thess.* 1:6–10).

God the Father, and Jesus Christ his Son, are for having things seen; for having the Word of life held forth. They light not a candle that it might be put under a bushel, or under a bed, but on a candlestick, that all that come in may see the light (*Matt.* 5:15; *Mark* 4:21; *Luke* 8:16; 11:33). And, I say, as I said before, in whom is it that light is so apt to shine as in the souls of great sinners?

When the Jewish Pharisees dallied with the gospel Christ threatened to take it from them and to give it to the barbarous heathens and idolaters. Why so? For they, said he, will bring forth the fruits thereof in their season. 'Therefore say I unto you, The kingdom of God shall be taken from you, and given to a nation bringing forth the fruits thereof' (*Matt.* 21:43).

I have often marvelled at our youth, and said in my heart, What should be the reason that they should be so generally debauched as they are at this day? For they are now amazingly profane; and sometimes I have thought one thing and sometimes another; that is, why God should suffer it so to be. At last I have thought of this: How if the God whose ways are past finding out should suffer it so to be now that he might make of some of them the more glorious saints hereafter? I know sin is of the devil, but it cannot work in the world without permission; and if it happens to be as I have thought, it will not be the first time that God the Lord has caught Satan in his own design. For my part, I believe that the time is at hand that we shall see better saints in the world than have been seen in it for many a day. And this vileness that at present does so much swallow up our youth is one cause of my thinking so; for out of them, for from among them, when God puts forth his hand, as of old, you shall see what penitent ones, what trembling ones, and what admirers of grace, will be found to profess the gospel, to the glory of God by Christ.

Alas! we are a company of worn-out Christians; our moon is in the wane; we are much more black than white, more dark than light; we shine but a little; grace in most of us is decayed. But I say, when those of these debauched ones that are to be saved shall be brought in – when these that look more like devils than men shall be converted to Christ (and I believe several of them will) – then will Christ be exalted, grace adored, the Word prized, Zion's path better trodden, and men in the pursuit of their own salvation, to the amazement of those that are left behind.

Just before Christ came in the flesh, the world was degenerated as it is now: the generality of the men in Jerusalem were become either high and famous for hypocrisy, or filthy and base in their lives. The devil also had broken loose in a hideous manner, and had taken possession of many: yea, I believe, that there was never a generation before or since that could produce so many possessed with devils, deformed, lame, blind, and infected with monstrous diseases as that generation could. But what was the reason thereof, I mean the reason from God? Why, one – and we may sum up more in that answer that Christ gave to his disciples concerning him that was born blind – was, that 'the works of God should be made manifest' in them, and 'that the Son of God might be glorified thereby' (*John* 9:2–3; 11:4).

Now, if these devils and diseases, as they possessed men then, were to make way and work for an approaching to Christ in person, and for the declaring of his power, why may we not think that now, even now also, he is ready to come by his Spirit in the gospel to heal many of the debaucheries of our age? I cannot believe that grace will take them all, for there are but few that are saved; but yet it will take some, even some of the worst of men, and make blessed ones of them. But, Oh, how these ringleaders in vice will then shine in virtue! They will be the very pillars in churches, they will be as an ensign in the land. 'The LORD their God shall save them in that day as the flock of his people: for they shall be as the stones of a crown, lifted up as an ensign upon his land' (*Zech.* 9:16). But who are these? Even idolatrous Ephraim, and backsliding Judah (verse 13).

I know there is ground to fear that the iniquity of this generation will be pursued with heavy judgments; but that will not hinder what we have supposed. God took a glorious church out of bloody Jerusalem, yea, out of the chief of the sinners there, and left the rest to be taken and spoiled, and sold, thirty for a penny, in the nations where they were captives. The gospel working gloriously in a place, to the seizing upon many of the ring-leading sinners thereof, promises no security to the rest, but rather threatens them with the heaviest and smartest judgments, as the instance just given fully demonstrates; but in defending, the Lord will defend his people; and in saving, he will save his inheritance. Nor does this speak any great comfort to a decayed and backsliding sort of Christians; for the next time God hastens with his gospel, he will leave such Christians behind him. But I say, Christ is resolved to set up his light in the world; yea, he is delighted to see his graces shine; and therefore he commands that his gospel should, to that end, be offered, in the first place, to the biggest sinners; for by great sins it shines most; therefore he says, 'Begin at Jerusalem.'

EIGHTH, and lastly, Christ Jesus will have mercy to be offered, in the first place, to the biggest sinners, because *by that means the impenitent that are left behind will be, at the judgment, the more left without excuse.*

God's Word has two edges; it can cut back-stroke and fore-stroke. If it does you no good, it will do you hurt; it is 'the savour of life unto life' to those that receive it, but of 'death unto death' to those that refuse it (2 *Cor.* 2:15–16). But this is not all; the offer of grace to the biggest sinners, in the first place, will not only leave the rest, or those that refuse it, in a deplorable condition, but will also stop their mouths and cut off all claim to any excuse at that day.

'If I had not come and spoken unto them,' says Christ, 'they had not had sin; but now they have no cloak for their sin' – for their sin of persevering in impenitence (*John* 15:22). But what did he speak to them? Why, even that which I have told you; namely, That he has a special delight in saving the biggest sinners. He spoke this in the way of his doctrine; he spoke it in the way of his practice, even to the extent of pouring out his last breath before them (*Luke* 23:34).

Now, since this is so, what can the condemned at the judgment say for themselves as to why sentence of death should not be passed upon them? I say, what excuse can they make for themselves, when they shall be asked why they did not, in the day of salvation, come to Christ to be saved? Will they have ground to say of the Lord, He was only for saving little sinners; and, therefore, because we were great ones, we dared not come to him; in that He had no compassion for the biggest sinners, therefore we died in despair? Will these be excuses for them, as the case now stands with them? Is there not everywhere in God's Book a flat contradiction to this, in multitudes of promises, of invitations, of examples, and the like? Alas! alas! there will then be there millions of souls to confute this plea; ready, I say, to stand up, and say, 'O! deceived world, heaven swarms with such as were, when they were in the world, fully as bad as you!' Now, this will kill all plea or excuse, why they should not perish in their sins; yea, the text says they shall see them there. 'There shall be weeping – when ye shall see Abraham, and Isaac, and

Jacob, and all the prophets, in the kingdom of heaven, and you yourselves thrust out. And they shall come from the east, and from the west, and from the north, and from the south, and shall sit down in the kingdom of God' (*Luke* 13:28–29). Out of this company it is easy to pick such as once were as bad people as any that now breathe on the face of the earth. What do you think of the first man, by whose sins there are millions now in hell? And so I may say, What do you think of ten thousand more besides?

But if the Word will not stifle and gag them up – I speak now to amplify the point – the view of those who are saved shall. There comes an incestuous person to the bar and pleads that the bigness of his sins was a bar to his receiving the promise. But will not his mouth be stopped as to that, when Lot, and the incestuous Corinthians, shall be set before him (*Gen.* 19:3–37; *1 Cor.* 5:1–2)?

There comes a thief, and says, Lord, my sin of theft, I thought, was such as could not be pardoned by thee! But when he shall see the thief that was saved on the cross stand by, as clothed with beauteous glory, what more can he object? Yet, the Lord will produce ten thousand of his saints at his coming who shall, after this manner, 'execute judgment upon all, and so convince all that are ungodly among them of all their hard speeches which ungodly sinners have spoken against him' (*Jude* 15). And these are hard speeches against him, to say that he was not able or willing to save men because of the greatness of their sins, or to say that they were discouraged by his Word from repentance, because of the heinousness of their offences. These things, I say, shall then be confuted. He comes with ten thousand of his saints to confute them, and to stop their mouths from making objections against their own eternal damnation.

Here is Adam, the destroyer of the world; here is Lot, that lay with both his daughters; here is Abraham, that was once an idolater; and Jacob, that was a supplanter; and Reuben, that lay with his father's concubine; and Judah, that lay with his daughter-in-law; and Levi and Simeon, that wickedly slew the Shechemites; and Aaron, that made an idol to be worshipped, and that proclaimed a religious feast unto it. Here is also Rahab the harlot, and Bathsheba that bare a bastard to David. Here is Solomon, that great backslider; and Manasseh, that man of blood, and a witch. Time would fail to tell you of the woman of Canaan's daughter, of Mary Magdalene, of Matthew the publican, and of Gideon and Samson, and many thousands more.

Alas! alas! I say, what will these sinners do, that have, through their unbelief, eclipsed the glorious largeness of the mercy of God, and given way to despair of salvation because of the bigness of their sins? For all these, though now glorious saints in light, were sometimes sinners of the biggest size, who had sins that were of a notorious hue; yet now, I say, they are in their shining and heavenly robes before the throne of God and of the Lamb, blessing for ever and ever that Son of God for their salvation, who died for them upon the tree; wondering that ever it should have come into their hearts once to think of coming to God by Christ; but above all, blessing God for granting them light to see those encouragements in his Testament without which, without doubt, they would have been daunted, and would have sunk down under the guilt of sin and despair, as their fellow-sinners have done. But now they also are witnesses for God, and for his grace, against an unbelieving world; for, as I said, they shall come to convince the world of their speeches, their hard and unbelieving words, that they have spoken concerning the mercy of God, and the merits of the passion of his blessed Son, Jesus Christ.

But do you not think it will strangely put to silence all such thoughts, and words, and reasons of the ungodly before the bar of God? Doubtless it will; and will send them away from his presence also with the greatest guilt that can possibly fasten upon the consciences of men.

For what will sting like this? – 'I have, through my own foolish, narrow, unworthy, undervaluing thoughts, of the love and ability of Christ to save me, brought myself to everlasting ruin. It is true, I was a horrible sinner; not one in a hundred did live so vile a life as I. But this should not have kept me from closing with Jesus Christ. I see now that there are abundance in glory that once were as bad as I have been; but they were saved by faith, and I am damned by unbelief. Wretch that I am! Why did not I give glory to the redeeming blood of Jesus? Why did I not humbly cast my soul at his blessed footstool for mercy? Why did I judge of his ability to save me by the voice of my shallow reason, and the voice of a guilty conscience? Why did I not betake myself to the holy Word of God? Why did I not read and pray that I might understand, since now I perceive that God said that He gives liberally to those that ask, and upbraids not (*James* 1:5).

It is rational to think that by such meditations as these the unbelieving world will be torn in pieces before the judgment of Christ; especially those that have lived where they did or might have heard the gospel of the grace of God. Oh! that saying, 'It shall be more tolerable for Sodom at the judgment than for them', will be better understood (see *Luke* 10:8–12.) This reason, therefore, stands fast; namely, that Christ by offering mercy, in the first place, to the biggest sinners now will stop all the mouths of the impenitent at the day of judgment, and cut off all excuse that shall be attempted on the grounds of the greatness of their sins as to why they came not to him.

I have often thought of the day of judgment and of how God will deal with sinners at that day; and I believe it will be managed with that sweetness, with that equitableness, with that excellent righteousness, as to every sin, and circumstance and aggravation thereof, that men that are damned shall, before the judgment is over, receive such conviction of the righteous judgment of God upon them, and of their deserts of hell-fire, that they shall in themselves conclude that there is all the reason in the world that they should be shut out of heaven, and go to hell-fire: 'These shall go away into everlasting punishment' (*Matt.* 25:46).

Only this will tear them, that they have missed mercy and glory, and obtained everlasting damnation, through their unbelief; but it will tear only themselves, only their own souls; they will gnash on themselves, in that mercy was offered to the chief of them in the first place, and yet they were damned for rejecting it; they were damned for forsaking what they had a propriety in; for forsaking their own mercy.

And thus much for the reasons why mercy is first offered to the biggest sinners, to the Jerusalem sinners. I will now conclude with a word of application.

3

The Doctrine Applied

IRST, would Jesus Christ have mercy offered, in the first place, to the biggest sinners? Then this shows us *how to make a right judgment of the heart of Christ to men.*

Indeed, we have advantage to guess at the goodness of his heart by many things, such as, by his taking our nature upon him, his dying for us, his sending his Word and ministers to us, all so that we might be saved. But this of beginning to offer mercy to Jerusalem is that which heightens all the rest; for this does not only confirm to us that love was the cause of his dying for us, but it shows us still more the depth of that love. He might have died for us, and yet have extended the benefit of his death to a few of the best-conditioned sinners, as one might call them, to those who, though they were weak, and so could not but sin, yet made not a trade of sinning; to those that sinned not extravagantly. There are in the world, as one may call them, the *moderate* sinners; the sinners that mix righteousness with their pollutions; the sinners that, though they are sinners, do what on their part lies – some that are blind would think so – that they might be saved. I say, it had been love, great love, if he had died for none but such, and sent his love to such; but that he should send out conditions of peace to the biggest of sinners, yea, that they should be offered to them first of all – (for so he means when he says, 'Begin at Jerusalem') – this is wonderful! this shows his heart to purpose, as also the heart of God his Father, who sent him to do thus.

There is nothing more natural to men that are awake in their souls, than to have wrong thoughts of God – thoughts that are narrow, and that pinch and pen up his mercy to scanty and beggarly conclusions, and rigid legal conditions; supposing that it is rude, and an intrenching upon his Majesty to come ourselves, or to invite others, until we have scraped and washed, and rubbed off as much of our dirt from us as we think is convenient, to make us somewhat orderly and handsome in his sight. Such never knew what these words meant, 'Begin at Jerusalem.' Yea, such in their hearts have compared the Father and his Son to niggardly rich men, whose money comes from them like drops of blood. True, say such, God has mercy, but he is loth to part with it; you must please him well, if you get any from him; he is not so free as many suppose, nor is he so willing to save as some pretended gospellers imagine.

But I ask such, if the Father and Son are not unspeakably free to show mercy, why was this clause put into our commission to preach the gospel? Yea, why did he say, 'Begin at Jerusalem': for when men, through the weakness of their wits, have attempted to show other reasons why they would have the first proffer of mercy, yet I can prove, by many undeniable reasons, that they of Jerusalem to whom the apostles made the first offer, as they were commanded, were the biggest sinners that ever did breathe upon the face of God's earth (set the unpardonable sin aside); upon which fact my doctrine stands like a rock, that Jesus the Son of God would have mercy, in the first place, offered to the biggest sinners. And if this does not show the heart of the Father and the Son to be infinitely free in bestowing forgiveness of sins, I confess myself mistaken.

Neither is there, set this aside, another argument like it, to show us the willingness of Christ to save sinners; for, as was said before, all the rest of the signs of Christ's mercifulness might have been limited to sinners that are so-and-so qualified; but when he says, 'Begin at Jerusalem', the line is stretched out to the utmost; no man can imagine beyond it; and it is folly here to pinch and spare, to narrow, and seek to bring it within scanty bounds; for he plainly says, 'Begin at Jerusalem', the biggest sinner is the biggest sinner; the biggest is the Jerusalem sinner.

It is true, he says that repentance and remission of sins must go together, but yet remission is sent to the chief, the Jerusalem sinner; nor does repentance lessen at all the Jerusalem sinner's crimes; it diminisheth none of his sins, nor causes that there should be so much as half a one the fewer; it only puts a stop to the Jerusalem sinner's course, and makes him willing to be saved freely by grace; and for time to come to be governed by that blessed Word that has brought the tidings of good things to him. Besides, no man shows himself willing to be saved that repents not of his deeds; for he that goes on still in his trespasses declares that he is resolved to pursue his own damnation further.

Learn then to judge of the largeness of God's heart, and of the heart of his Son Jesus Christ, by the Word; judge not thereof by feeling, nor by the reports of conscience; conscience is oftentimes here befooled, and made to go quite astray from the Word. It was judging without the Word that made David say, 'I am cut off from before thine eyes', and 'I shall now perish one day by the hand of Saul' (*Psa.* 31:22; *1 Sam.* 27:1). The Word had told him another thing; namely, that he should be king in his stead. Our text says also that Jesus Christ bids preachers, in their preaching repentance and remission of sins, to begin at Jerusalem; thereby declaring most truly the infinite largeness of the merciful heart of God and his Son, to the sinful children of men. Judge, I say, therefore, of the goodness of the heart of God and his Son by this text, and by others of the same import; so shall you not dishonour the grace of God, nor needlessly affright yourself, nor give away your faith, nor gratify the devil, nor lose the benefit of God's Word. I speak now to weak believers.

SECOND, Would Jesus Christ have mercy offered, in the first place, to the biggest sinners, to the Jerusalem sinners?

Then, by this also you must learn to judge of the suffi- ciency of the merits of Christ; not that the merits of Christ can be comprehended, for they are beyond the concep- tions of the whole world, being called 'the unsearchable riches of Christ'; but yet they may be apprehended to a considerable degree. Now, the way to apprehend them most is to consider what offers, after his resurrection, he makes of his grace to sinners; for to be sure he will not offer beyond the virtue of his merits; because, as grace is the cause of his merits, so his merits are the basis and bounds upon and by which his grace stands good, and is let out to sinners.

Does he then command that his mercy should be offered, in the first place, to the biggest sinners? This declares that there is a sufficiency in his blood to save the biggest sinners. 'The blood of Jesus Christ cleanseth from all sin.' And again, 'Be it known unto you therefore, men and brethren, that through this man [this man's merits] is preached unto you the forgiveness of sins; and by him all that believe are justified from all things, from which ye could not be justified by the law of Moses' (*Acts* 13: 38–39).

Observe, then, this rule to make judgment of the suffi- ciency of the blessed merits of your Saviour. If he had not been able to reconcile the biggest sinners to his Father by his blood, he would not have sent to them, have sent to them *in the first place*, the doctrine of remission of sins; for remission of sins is through faith in his blood. We are justified freely by the grace of God, through the redemption that is in the blood of Christ. Upon the stand-ard, as I may call it, of the worthiness of the blood of Christ, grace acts, and offers forgiveness of sin to men (*Eph.* 1:7; 2:13–14; *Col.* 1:20–22). Hence, therefore, we must gather, that the blood of Christ is of infinite value, because he offers mercy to the biggest of sinners.

Nay, further, since he offers mercy, in the first place, to the biggest sinners, consider also, that this first act of his is that which the world will take notice of, and expect it should be continued unto the end. It is a disparagement to a man that seeks his own glory in what he undertakes to do that for a spurt which he cannot continue and hold out in. This is our Lord's own argument, He began to build, says he, but was not able to finish (*Luke* 14:30).

If you should hear a man say, I am resolved to be kind to the poor, and he should begin by giving handfuls of guineas, you would conclude that, either he is wonder-fully rich, or he must limit his giving or he will soon be at the bottom of his riches. Why, this is the case: Christ, at his resurrection, gave it out that he would be good to the world; and first sends to the biggest sinners, with an intent to have mercy on them. Now, the biggest sinners cannot be saved but by abundance of grace; it is not a little that will save great sinners (*Rom.* 5:17). And I say again, since the Lord Jesus mounts thus high at the first, and sends to the Jerusalem sinners that they may come first to partake of his mercy, it follows that, either he has unsearchable riches of grace and worth in himself, or else he must limit his giving, or his grace and merits will be spent before the world is at an end. But let it be believed, as surely as spoken, he is still as full as ever. He is not a jot the poorer for all the forgiveness that he has given away to great sinners. Also he is still as free as at first; for he never yet called back this word, Begin at the Jerusalem sinners. And, as I said, since his grace is extended according to the worth of his merits, I conclude, that there is the same virtue in his merits to save now, as there was at the very beginning, Oh! the riches of the grace of Christ! Oh! the riches of the blood of Christ!

THIRD, Would Jesus Christ have mercy offered in the first place to the biggest sinners? Then *here is encouragement for you that think that, for wicked hearts and lives, you have not your equals in the world, still to come to him.*

There is a people that fear lest they should be rejected by Jesus Christ because of the greatness of their sins; whereas, as you see here, such are sent to, sent to by Jesus Christ, to come to him for mercy: 'Begin at Jerusalem.' Never did one thing answer another more fitly in this world than this text fits this kind of sinner. As face answers face in a glass, so this text answers the necessities of such sinners. What can a man say more, but that he stands in the rank of the biggest sinners? Let him stretch himself as far as he can, and think of himself to the utmost, he can but conclude himself to be one of the biggest sinners. And what then? Why, the text meets him in the very face and says, Christ offers mercy to the biggest

[69]

sinners, to the very Jerusalem sinners. What more can be objected? Nay, he does not only offer such his mercy, but it is commanded to be offered to them *in the first place*: 'Begin at Jerusalem.' 'Preach repentance and remission of sins among all nations: beginning at Jerusalem.' Is there not here encouragement for those that think that, for wicked hearts and lives, they have not their equals in the world?

Objection: But I have a heart as hard as a rock.

Answer: Well, but this does but prove you one of the biggest sinners.

Objection: But my heart continually frets against the Lord.

Answer: Well, this does but prove you one of the biggest sinners.

Objection: But I have been desperate in sinful courses.

Answer: Well, stand with the number of the biggest sinners.

Objection: But my grey head is found in the way of wickedness.

Answer: Well, you are in the rank of the biggest sinners.

Objection: But I have not only a base heart, but I have lived a debauched life.

Answer: Stand also among those that are called the biggest sinners. And what then? Why, the text swoops you all; you cannot object that you are beyond the text. It has a particular message to the biggest sinners. I say, it swoops you all.[1]

---

[1] It seizes you as a hawk does its prey.

Objection: But I am a reprobate.

Answer: Now you are talking like a fool, and meddling with what you understand not: no sin but the sin of final impenitence can prove a man a reprobate; and I am sure you have not yet arrived at that; therefore you understand not what you are saying, and make groundless conclusions against yourself. Say you are a sinner, and I will hold with you, say you are a great sinner, and I will say so too; yes, say you are one of the biggest sinners, and spare not; for the text is still beyond you. It is still between hell and you.

'Begin at Jerusalem' still smiles upon you; and you talk as if you were a reprobate, and as if the greatness of your sins proved you so to be, when yet they of Jerusalem were not such, whose sins, I dare say, were such, both for bigness and heinousness, as you are not capable of committing beyond them; unless now, after you have received conviction that the Lord Jesus is the only Saviour of the world, you should wickedly and despitefully turn from him, and conclude he is not to be trusted to for life, and so crucify him for a cheat afresh.

This, I must confess, will bring a man under the black rod, and set him in danger of eternal damnation (*Heb.* 6:7; 10:8–9). This is trampling under foot the Son of God, and counting his blood an unholy thing. This those of Jerusalem did; but they did it ignorantly, in unbelief, and so were yet capable of mercy; but to do this against professed light, and to stand to it, puts a man beyond the text indeed (*Acts* 3:14–17; *1 Tim.* 1:13).

But I say, what is this to him that would happily be saved by Christ? His sins did, as to greatness, never yet reach to the nature of the sins that the sinners intended by the text had made themselves guilty of. He that would be saved by Christ has an honourable esteem of him; but those of Jerusalem preferred a murderer before him; and as for him, they cried, Away, away with him, it is not fit that he should live. Perhaps you will object that you have a thousand times preferred a stinking lust before him. I answer, Be it so; it is but what is common to men to do; nor does the Lord Jesus make such a foolish life a bar to you, to forbid your coming to him, or a bond to his grace, that it might be kept from you; but he admits your repentance, and offers himself to you freely, as you stand among the Jerusalem sinners.

Therefore take encouragement, man; mercy is, by the text, held forth to the biggest sinners; yea, put yourself into the number of the worst by reckoning that you may be one of the first, and may not be put off till the biggest sinners are served; for the biggest sinners are first invited; consequently, if they come, they are likely to be the first that shall be served. It was so with Jerusalem; Jerusalem sinners were they that were first invited, and those of them that came first – and there came three thousand of them the first day they were invited; how many came afterwards none can tell – they were first served.

Put in your name, man, among the biggest, lest you should be made to wait till they are served. You have some men that think themselves very cunning because they put up their names in their prayers among those who make a show of it, saying, God, I thank thee I am not so bad as the worst. But believe it, if they are saved at all, they shall be saved in the last place. The first in their own eyes shall be served last; and the last or worst shall be first. The text insinuates it, 'Begin at Jerusalem'; and reason backs it, for they have most need. Behold, therefore, how God's ways are above ours; we are for serving the worst last, God is for serving the worst first. The man at the pool that, to my thinking, was longest in his disease and most helpless as to a cure was first healed; yea, he alone was healed; for we read that Christ healed him, but we read not then that he healed one more there (*John* 5: 1–10)! Wherefore, if you would be served soonest , put in your name among the very worst of sinners. Say, when you are upon your knees, Lord, here is a Jerusalem sinner! A sinner of the biggest size! One whose burden is of the greatest bulk and heaviest weight! One that cannot stand long without sinking into hell, without thy supporting hand! 'Be not thou far from me, O LORD; O my strength, haste thee to help me' (*Psa.* 22:19)!

I say, put in your name with Magdalene, with Manasseh, that you may fare as the Magdalene and the Manasseh sinners do. The man in the gospel made the desperate condition of his child an argument with Christ to haste his cure: 'Sir, come down', said he, 'ere my child die' (*John* 4:49), and Christ regarded his haste, saying, 'Go thy way; thy son liveth' (verse 50). Haste requires haste. David was for speed; 'Deliver me speedily'; 'Hear me speedily'; 'Answer me speedily' (*Psa.* 31:2; 69:17; 102:2). But why speedily? I am in 'the net'; 'I am in trouble'; 'My days are consumed like smoke' (*Psa.* 31:4; 69:17; 102:3). 'Deep calleth unto deep'; necessity calls for help; great necessity for present help. Wherefore, I say, be ruled by me in this matter; feign not yourself another man, if you have been a filthy sinner, but go in your own colours to Jesus Christ, and put yourself among the most vile, and leave him to 'put you among the children' (*Jer.* 3:19).

Confess all that you know of yourself; I know you will find it hard work to do thus, especially if your mind is legal; but do it, lest you stay and be deferred with the little sinners, until the great ones have had their alms. What do you think David intended when he said, his wounds stank and were corrupt, but to hasten God to have mercy upon him, and not to defer his cure? 'Lord,' says he, 'I am troubled; I am bowed down greatly; I go mourning all the day long.' 'I am feeble and sore broken: I have roared by reason of the disquietness of my heart' (*Psa.* 38:6, 8). David knew what he did by all this; he knew that his making the worst of his case, was the way to speedy help, and that a feigning and dissembling the matter with God was the shortest way to put a stop to his forgiveness.

I have one thing more to offer for the encouragement of the one who deems himself one of the biggest sinners; and that is, you are as it were called by name, in the first place, to come in for mercy. Man of Jerusalem, hearken to the call; men do so in courts of judicature, and presently cry out, 'Here, Sir'; and then they shoulder and crowd, and say, 'Pray give way, I am called into the court.' Why, this is your case, great sinner, Jerusalem sinner; be of good cheer, he calls you (*Mark* 10:46–49). Why sit still? arise: why stand still? come, man, the call should give you authority to come. 'Begin at Jerusalem', is your call and authority to come; wherefore up and shoulder it, man; say, 'Stand away, devil, Christ calls me; stand away unbelief, Christ calls me; stand away, all my discouraging apprehensions, for my Saviour calls me to him to receive of his mercy.' Men will do thus, as I said, in courts below; and why should you not approach thus to the court above? The Jerusalem sinner is first in thought, first in commission, first in the record of names; and therefore should give attendance, with the expectation that he is first to receive mercy of God.

Is not this an encouragement to the biggest sinners to make their application to Christ for mercy? 'Come unto me, all ye that labour and are heavy laden', also confirms this thing; that is, that the biggest sinner, and he that has the biggest burden, is he who is first invited. Christ points over the heads of thousands, as he sits on the throne of grace, directly to such a man; and says, 'Bring in hither the maimed, the halt, and the blind; let the Jerusalem sinner that stands there behind come to me.' Wherefore, since Christ says, 'Come,' to you, let the angels make a lane, and let all men give place, that the Jerusalem sinner may come to Jesus Christ for mercy.

FOURTH, Would Jesus Christ have mercy offered, in the first place, to the biggest sinners? Then come, profane wretch, and *let me a little enter into an argument with you.* Why will you not come to Jesus Christ, since you are a Jerusalem sinner? How can you find in your heart to set yourself against grace, against such grace as offers mercy to you? What spirit possesses you, and holds you back from a sincere closure with your Saviour? Behold, God groaningly complains of you, saying, 'But Israel would none of me.' 'When I called, none did answer' (*Psa.* 81:11; *Isa.* 66:4).

Shall God enter this complaint against you? Why do you put him off? Why do you stop your ear? Can you defend yourself? When you are called to an account for your neglects of so great salvation, what can you answer? or do you think that you shall escape the judgment? (*Heb.* 2:3). No more such Christs! There will be no more such Christs, sinner! Oh, put not the day, the day of grace, away from you! If it be once gone, it will never come again, sinner.

But what is it that has got your heart, and that keeps it from your Saviour? 'Who in the heaven can be compared unto the LORD? who among the sons of the mighty can be likened unto the LORD?' (*Psa.* 89:6). Have you, do you think, found anything so good as Jesus Christ? Is there any among your sins, your companions, and foolish delights, that, like Christ, can help you in the day of your distress? Behold, the greatness of your sins cannot hinder; let not the stubbornness of your heart hinder you, sinner.

Objection: I am ashamed.

Answer: Oh! don't be ashamed to be saved, sinner.

Objection: But my old companions will mock me.

Answer: Oh! don't be mocked out of eternal life, sinner.

Your stubborness affects, afflicts the heart of your Saviour. Do you not care for this? Of old, 'he beheld the city, and wept over it.' Can you hear this, and not be concerned (*Luke* 19:41–42)? Shall Christ weep to see your soul going on to destruction, and will you sport yourself in that way? Yea, shall Christ, that can be eternally happy without you, be more afflicted at the thoughts of the loss of your soul, than yourself, who are certainly eternally miserable if you neglect to come to him? Those things that keep you and your Saviour, on your part, asunder, are but bubbles; the least prick of an affliction will let out, as to you, what now you think is worth the venture of heaven to enjoy.

Have you not reason? Can you not so much as once soberly think of your dying hour, or of whither your sinful life will drive you then? Have you no conscience? or having one, is it rocked so fast asleep by sin, or made so weary with unsuccessful calling upon you, that it is laid down, and cares for you no more? Poor man! your state is to be lamented. Have you no judgment? Are you not able to conclude that to be saved is better than to burn in hell? and that eternal life with God's favour, is better than a temporal life in God's displeasure? Have you no affection but what is brutish? What, none at all? No affection for the God that made you? What! none for his loving

Son that has showed his love, and died for you? Is not heaven worth your affection? O poor man! which is strongest, think you, God or you? If you are not able to overcome him, you are a fool for standing out against him (*Matt.* 5:25–26). 'It is a fearful thing to fall into the hand of the living God' (*Heb.* 10:29–31). He will grip hard; his fist is stronger than a lion's paw; take heed of him, he will be angry if you despise his Son; and will you stand guilty in your trespasses, when he offers you his grace and favour (*Exod.* 34:6–7)?

Now we come to the text, 'Beginning at Jerusalem.' This text, though it be now one of the brightest stars that shine in the Bible, because there is in it as full, if not the fullest, offer of grace that can be imagined to the sons of men; yet, to them that shall perish from under this word, even this text will be to such one of the hottest coals in hell. This text, therefore, will save you or sink you: there is no shifting of it; if it saves you, it will set you high; if it sinks you, it will set you low.

But, I say, why so unconcerned? Have you no soul? or do you think you may lose your soul, and save yourself? Is it not a pity, had it otherwise been the will of God, that ever you were made a man, in that you set so little by your soul? Sinner, take the invitation; you are called upon to come to Christ: nor are you called upon but by order from the Son of God, though you should happen to come of the biggest sinners; for he has bid us offer mercy, as to all the world in general, so, in the first place, to the sinners of Jerusalem, or to the biggest sinners.

FIFTH, Would Jesus Christ have mercy offered, in the first place, to the biggest sinners? Then, *this shows how unreasonable a thing it is for men to despair of mercy;* as for those that presume, I shall say something to them afterwards.

I now speak to those that despair. There are four sorts of despair. There is the despair of devils; there is the despair of souls in hell; there is the despair that is grounded upon men's deficiency; and there is the despair that they are perplexed with that are willing to be saved, but are too strongly borne down with the burden of their sins.

The despair of devils, the damned's despair, and that despair that a man has of attaining life because of his own deficiency are all reasonable. Why should not devils and damned souls despair? yea, why should not man despair of getting to heaven by his own abilities? I, therefore, am concerned only with the fourth sort of despair, to wit, with *the despair of those that would be saved, but are too strongly borne down with the burden of their sins.* I say, therefore, to you that are thus, And why despair? Your despair, if it was reasonable, should flow from you, because found in the land that is beyond the grave; or because you certainly know that Christ will not, or cannot save you.

But, for the first, you are yet in the land of the living; and, for the second, you have ground to believe quite the contrary; Christ is able to save to the uttermost them that come to God by him; and if he were not willing, he would not have commanded that mercy, in the first place, should be offered to the biggest sinners. Besides, he has said, 'And let him that is athirst come. And whosoever will, let him take the water of life *freely*'; that is, *with all my heart*. What ground now is here for despair? If you say, The number and burden of my sins, I answer, Nay; that is rather a ground for faith; because such a one, above all others, is invited by Christ to come to him, yea, promised rest and forgiveness if they come (*Matt.* 11:28). What ground then to despair? Truly, none at all. Your despair, then, is a thing unreasonable, and without footing in the Word.

'But I have no experience of God's love; God has given me no comfort, or ground of hope, though I have waited upon him for it many a day.' You have experience of God's love, in that he has opened your eyes to see your sins, and in that he has given you desires to be saved by Jesus Christ. For by your sense of sin you are made to see your poverty of spirit, and that has laid under you a sure ground to hope that heaven shall be yours hereafter.

Also your desires to be saved by Christ have put you under another promise, so there are two to hold you up in hope, though your present burden be never so heavy (*Matt.* 5:3,6). As for what you say of God's silence to you, perhaps he has spoken to you once or twice already, but you have not perceived it (*Job* 33:14–15). However, you have Christ crucified set forth before your eyes in the Bible, and an invitation to come to him, though you be a Jerusalem sinner, though you be one of the biggest sinners; and so you have no ground to despair. What if God will be silent to you, is that ground of despair? Not at all, so long as there is a promise in the Bible, that God will in no wise cast away the coming sinner, and so long as he invites the Jerusalem sinner to come unto him (*John* 6:37).

Build not, therefore, despair upon these things; they are no sufficient foundation for it, such plenty of promises being in the Bible, and such a discovery of his mercy to great sinners of old; especially since we have also a clause in the commission given to ministers to preach, that they should begin with the Jerusalem sinners in their offering of mercy to the world. Besides, God says, 'They that wait upon the LORD shall renew their strength, they shall mount up with wings like eagles'; but, perhaps, it may be long first. I waited long, says David, and did seek the Lord; and, at length, his cry was heard: wherefore he bids his soul wait on God, and says, For it is good so to do before thy saints (*Psa.* 40:1; 62:5; 52:9).

And what if you wait upon God all your days? Is it below you? And what if God will cross his book, and blot out the handwriting that is against you, and not let you know it as yet? Is it fit to say to God, You are hard-hearted? Despair not; you have no ground to despair, so long as you live in this world. It is a sin to begin to despair before one sets his foot over the threshold of hell-gates. For them that are there, let them despair and spare not; but as for you, you have no ground to do it. What! despair of bread in a land that is full of corn! Despair of mercy when our God is full of mercy! Despair of mercy, when God goes about, by his ministers, beseeching sinners to be reconciled unto him (2 *Cor.* 5:18–20)! You scrupulous fool, where can you find that God was ever false to his promise, or that he ever deceived the soul that ventured itself upon him? He often calls upon sinners to trust him, though they walk in darkness, and have no light (*Isa.* 50:10). They have his promise and oath for their salvation, that flee for refuge to the hope set before them (*Heb.* 6:17–18).

Despair! when we have a God of mercy, and a redeeming Christ alive! For shame, forbear; let them despair that dwell where there is no God, and that are confined to those chambers of death which can be reached by no redemption. A living man despair when he is reproved for murmuring and complaining (*Lam.* 3:39)! Oh! so long as we are where promises swarm, where mercy is proclaimed, where grace reigns, and where Jerusalem sinners are privileged with the first offer of mercy, it is a base thing to despair. Despair undervalues the promise, undervalues the invitation, undervalues the proffer of grace. Despair undervalues the ability of God the Father, and the redeeming blood of Christ his Son. Oh, unreasonable despair! Despair makes man God's judge; it is a controller of the promise, a contradictor of Christ in his large offers of mercy: and one that undertakes to make unbelief the great manager of our reason and judgment, in determining about what God can and will do for sinners. Despair! It is the devil's fellow, the devil's master; yea, the chains with which he is captivated and held under darkness for ever: and to give way thereto in a land, in a state and time, that flows with milk and honey is an uncomely thing.

I would say to my soul, 'O my soul! this is not the place of despair; this is not the time to despair in; as long as mine eyes can find a promise in the Bible, as long as there is the least mention of grace, as long as there is a moment left me of breath or life in this world, so long will I wait or look for mercy, so long will I fight against unbelief and despair.' This is the way to honour God and Christ; this is the way to set the crown on the promise; this is the way to welcome the invitation and Inviter; and this is the way to thrust yourself under the shelter and protection of the Word of grace. Never despair so long as our text is alive, for that does sound it out – that mercy by Christ is offered, in the first place, to the biggest sinner.

Despair is an unprofitable thing; it will make a man weary of waiting upon God (2 *Kings* 6:33). It will make a man forsake God, and seek his heaven in the good things of this world (*Gen.* 4:13–18). It will make a man his own tormentor, and flounce and fling like 'a wild bull in a net' (*Isa.* 51:20). Despair! it drives a man to the study of his own ruin, and brings him at last to be his own executioner (2 *Sam.* 17:23; *Matt.* 27:3–5).

Besides, I am persuaded also, that despair is the cause that there are so many that desire to be atheists in the world. For, because they have entertained a conceit that God will never be merciful to them, therefore they labour to persuade themselves that there is no God at all, as if their disbelief would kill God, or cause him to cease to be. A poor shift for an immortal soul, for a soul which does not like to retain God in its knowledge! If this is the best that despair can do, let it go, man, and betake yourself to faith, to prayer, to waiting for God, and to hope, despite ten thousand doubts. And for your encouragement, take yet, as an addition to what has already been said, the following Scripture: 'The LORD taketh pleasure in them that fear him, in those that hope in his mercy' (*Psa.* 147:11). From this note, they fear not God that hope not in his mercy; also, God is angry with them that do not hope in his mercy; for he only takes pleasure in those that hope. 'He that believeth', or 'hath received his testimony, hath set to his seal that God is true' (*John* 3:33). But he that receives it not 'hath made him a liar', and that is a very unworthy thing (*1 John* 5:10–11).

'Let the wicked forsake his way, and the unrighteous man his thoughts: and let him return unto the LORD, and he will have mercy upon him; and to our God, for he will abundantly pardon' (*Isa.* 55:7). Perhaps you are weary of your ways, but are not weary of your thoughts; of your unbelieving and despairing thoughts; now, God also would have you cast away these thoughts, as things which he does not deserve at your hands; for 'he will have mercy upon you, and he will abundantly pardon'.

'O fools, and slow of heart to believe all that the prophets have spoken!' (*Luke* 24:25). Mark here, slowness to believe is a piece of folly. Aye! but do you say, I do believe *some*, and I believe what goes against me. Aye but, sinner,

Christ Jesus here calls you a fool for not believing *all*. Believe all, and despair if you can! He that believes all believes that text that says Christ would have mercy preached first to the Jerusalem sinners. He that believes all believes all the promises and consolations of the Word; and the promises and consolations of the Word weigh heavier than do all the curses and threatenings of the law; and mercy rejoices against judgment. Therefore, believe all, and mercy will, to your conscience, weigh judgment down, and so minister comfort to your soul. The Lord take the yoke from off your jaws, since he has set meat before you (*Hos.* 11:4), and help you to remember that he is pleased, in the first place, to offer mercy to the biggest sinners.

Sixth, Since Jesus Christ would have mercy offered, in the first place, to the biggest sinners, *let souls see that they rightly lay hold of it lest they, notwithstanding, indeed come short of it.*

Faith alone knows how to deal with mercy; wherefore, put not presumption in the place thereof. I have observed that, as there are herbs and flowers in our gardens, so there are their counterfeits in the field; only they are distinguished from the other by the name of *wild* ones. Why, there is faith, and wild faith; and wild faith is this presumption. I call it *wild faith*, because God never placed it in his garden – his church; it is only to be found in the field – the world. I also call it wild faith, because it only grows up and is nourished where other wild notions abound. Wherefore, take heed of this, and all may be well; for this presumptuousness is a very heinous thing in the eyes of God. 'The soul', says he, 'that doeth ought presumptuously, whether he be born in the land, or a stranger, the same reproacheth the LORD; and that soul shall be cut off from among his people' (*Num.* 15:30).

The thoughts of this made David tremble, and pray that God would hold him back from presumptuous sins, and not suffer them to have dominion over him (*Psa.* 19:13). Now this presumption puts itself in the place of faith when it tampers with the promise of life while the soul is a stranger to repentance. Therefore, you have in the text, to prevent doing this, both repentance and remission of sins to be offered to Jerusalem; not remission without repentance, for all that repent not shall perish, let them presume on grace and the promise while they will (*Luke* 13:1–3).

Presumption, then, is that which severs faith and repentance, concluding that the soul shall be saved by grace, though the man was never made sorry for his sins, nor the love of the heart turned therefrom. This is to be self-willed, as Peter has it; and this is a despising of the Word of the Lord, for that has put repentance and faith together (*Mark* 1:15). And 'because he hath despised the word of the LORD, and hath broken his commandment, that soul shall utterly be cut off; his iniquity shall be upon him' (*Num.* 15:31). Let such, therefore, look to it who yet are, and abide, in their sins; for such, if they hope, as they are, to be saved, presume upon the grace of God. Wherefore, presumption and not hearkening to God's Word are put together (*Deut.* 17:12).

Again, men presume, when they are resolved to abide in their sins, and yet expect to be saved by God's grace through Christ. This is as much as to say, God favours sin as much as I do, and cares not how men live, so long as they lean upon his Son. Of this sort are they 'that build up Zion with blood, and Jerusalem with iniquity'; that 'judge for reward, and teach for hire, and divine for money, and lean upon the Lord' (*Mic.* 3:10–11).

This is doing things with a high hand against the Lord our God, and taking him, as it were, at the catch. This is, as we say among men, to seek to put a trick upon God; as if he had not sufficiently fortified his proposals of grace, by his holy Word, against all such kind of fools as these. But look to it! Such will be found at the day of God, not among that great company of Jerusalem sinners that shall be saved by grace, but among those that have been the great abusers of the grace of God in the world. Those that say, Let us sin that grace may abound, and let us do evil that good may come, their damnation is just. And if so, they are a great way off from that salvation that is by Jesus Christ presented to the Jerusalem sinners.

I have, therefore, these things to propound to that Jerusalem sinner that would know if he may be so bold as to venture himself upon this grace. 1. *Do you see your sins?* 2. *Are you weary of them?* 3. *Would you, with all your heart, be saved by Jesus Christ?* I dare say no less; I dare say no more. But if it be truly thus with you, how great soever your sins have been, how bad soever you feel your heart, how far soever you are from thinking that God has mercy for you, you are the man, the Jerusalem sinner, that the Word of God has conquered, and to whom it offers free remission of sins, by the redemption that is in Jesus Christ.

When the jailor cried out, 'Sirs, what must I do to be saved?' the answer was, 'Believe on the Lord Jesus Christ, and thou shalt be saved.' He that sees his sins aright is brought to his wit's end by them; and he that is so is willing to part from them and to be saved by the grace of God. If this be your case, fear not, give no way to despair; you presume not if you believe to life everlasting in Jesus Christ; yea, Christ is prepared for such as you are. Therefore, take good courage, and believe.

The design of Satan is to tell the presumptuous that their presuming on mercy is good; but to persuade the believer that his believing is impudent, bold dealing with God. I never heard a presumptuous man, in my life, say that he was afraid that he presumed; but I have heard many an honest humble soul say that they have been afraid that their faith has been presumption. Why should Satan molest those whose ways he knows will bring them to him? And who can think that he should be quiet when men take the right course to escape his hellish snares? This, therefore, is the reason why the truly humbled is opposed, while the presumptuous goes on by wind and tide. The truly humble Satan hates; but he laughs to see the foolery of the other.

Do your hand and heart tremble? Upon you the promise smiles. 'To this man will I look,' says God, 'even to him that is poor and of a contrite spirit, and trembleth at my word' (*Isa.* 66:2). What, therefore, I have said of presumption concerns not the humble in spirit at all. I therefore am for gathering up the stones, and for taking the stumbling blocks out of the way of God's people; and for warning those that lay the stumbling block of their iniquity before their faces, and those that are for presuming upon God's mercy: let them look to themselves (*Ezek.* 14:6–8).

Also, our text stands firm as ever it did, and our observation is still of force, that Jesus Christ would have mercy offered, in the first place, to the biggest sinners. So then, let none despair, let none presume; let none despair that are sorry for their sins, and would be saved by Jesus Christ; let none presume that abide in the liking of their sins, though they seem to know the exceeding grace of Christ. For though the door stands wide open for the reception of the penitent, yet it is fast enough barred and bolted against the presumptuous sinner. Be not deceived, God is not mocked: whatsoever a man sows, that he shall reap. It cannot be that God should be wheedled out of his mercy, or prevailed upon by lips of dissimulation; he knows them that trust in him, and that sincerely come to him by Christ for mercy (*Nahum* 1:7).

It is, then, not the abundance of sins committed, but the not coming heartily to God by Christ for mercy, that shuts men out of doors. And though their not coming heartily may be said to be but a sin, yet it is such a sin as causes that all your other sins abide upon you unforgiven. God complains of this. 'They have not cried unto me with their heart . . . they return, but not to the most High' (*Hos.* 7:14, 16) They turned 'feignedly' (*Jer.* 3:10). Thus doing, his soul hates them; but the penitent, humble, broken-hearted sinner, be his transgressions red as scarlet, red like crimson, in number as the sand; though his transgressions cry to heaven against him for vengeance, and seem there to cry louder than do his prayers, or tears, or groans for mercy; yet he is safe. To this man God will look (*Isa.* 1:18; 66:2).

SEVENTH, Would Jesus Christ have mercy offered, in the first place, to the biggest sinners? Then *here is ground for those that, as to practice, have not been such to come to him for mercy.*

Although there is no sin little of itself, because it is a contradiction of the nature and majesty of God, yet we must distinguish numbers, and also aggravations. Two sins are not so many as three; nor are three that are done in ignorance as big as one that is done against light, knowledge, and conscience. Also, there is the child in sin, and a man in sin that has grey hair and his skin wrinkled for very age. And we must put a difference between these sinners also; for can it be that a child of seven, or ten, or sixteen years old, should be such a sinner – a sinner so vile in the eyes of the law as he is who has walked according to the course of this world, forty, fifty, sixty, or seventy years? Now, the youth, this stripling, though he is a sinner, is but a little sinner when compared with such. Now, I say, *if there is room for the first sort, for those of the biggest size, certainly there is room for the lesser size.* If there is a door wide enough for a giant to go in at, there is certainly room for a dwarf. If Christ Jesus has grace enough to save great sinners, he has surely grace enough to save little ones. If he can forgive five hundred pence, for certain he can forgive fifty (*Luke* 7:41–42).

'But you said before, that the little sinners must stand by until the great ones have received their grace, and that is discouraging!' I answer, there are two sorts of little sinners – such as *are* so, and such as *feign themselves* so. It was those that feign themselves so that I intended there, and not those that are, indeed, comparatively so. Such as feign themselves so may wait long enough before they obtain forgiveness.

But again, a sinner may be comparatively a little sinner, and sensibly a great one. There are, then, two sorts of greatness in sin – greatness by reason of number, and greatness by reason of thoroughness of conviction of the horrible nature of sin. In this last sense, he that sins but one sin, if such a one could be found, may, in his own eyes, find himself the biggest sinner in the world. Let this man or this child, therefore, put himself among the great sinners, and plead with God as great sinners do, and expect to be saved with the great sinners, and as soon and as heartily as they. Yea, a little sinner, that, comparatively, is truly so, if he shall graciously give way to conviction, and shall, in God's light, diligently weigh the horrible nature of his own sins, may yet sooner obtain forgiveness for them at the hands of the heavenly Father, than he that has ten times his sins, and so has cause to cry ten times harder to God for mercy.

For the grievousness of the cry is a great thing with God; for if he will hear the widow, if she cries at all, how much more if she cries most grievously (*Exod.* 22:22–23)? It is not the number but the true sense of the abominable nature of sin that makes the cry for pardon lamentable. He, as I said, that has many sins, may not cry so loud in the ears of God as he that has far fewer; he, in our present sense, that is in his own eyes the biggest sinner, is he that soonest finds mercy. The offer, then, is to the biggest sinner; to the biggest sinner first, and the mercy is first obtained by him that first confesseth himself to be such a one.

There are men that strive at the throne of grace for mercy by pleading the greatness of their necessity. Now their plea, as to the prevalency of it, lies not in their counting up the number but in their sense of the greatness of their sins, and in the vehemency of their cry for pardon. And it is observable that though the birthright was Reuben's and, for his foolishness, given to the sons of Joseph, yet Judah prevailed above his brethren, and of him came the Messiah (*1 Chron.* 5:1–2). There is a heavenly subtlety to be managed in this matter. 'Thy brother came with subtlety, and hath taken away thy blessing.' The blessing belonged to Esau, but Jacob by his diligence made it his own (*Gen.* 27:35). The offer is to the biggest sinner, to the biggest sinner first; but if he forbears to cry, the sinner that is a sinner less by far than he, both as to the number and nature of transgressions, may get the blessing first, if he shall have grace to bestir himself well; for the loudest cry is heard furthest, and the most lamentable pierces soonest.

I therefore urge this head, not because I would have little sinners go and tell God that they are little sinners, thereby thinking to obtain his mercy; for truly so they are never likely to have it; for such words declare that such a one has no true sense at all of the nature of his sins. Sin, as I said, in the nature of it is horrible, though it be but one single act; yea, though it be but a sinful thought; and so worthily calls for the damnation of the soul. The comparison, then, of little and great sinners is to go for good sense among men. But to plead the fewness of your sins, or the comparative harmlessness of their quantity before God, argues no sound knowledge of the nature of your sin, and so no true sense of the nature or need of mercy.

Little sinner! When therefore you go to God, though you know in your conscience that you, as to acts, are no thief, no murderer, no whore, no liar, no false swearer, or the like, and in reason must needs understand that thus you are not so profanely vile as others; yet when you go to God for mercy, know no man's sins but your own, make mention of no man's sins but your own. Also labour not to lessen your own, but magnify and enlarge them by all just circumstances, and be as if there was never a sinner in the world but yourself. Also cry out as if you were the only undone man; and that is the way to obtain God's mercy.

It is one of the comeliest sights in the world to see a little sinner commenting on the greatness of his sins, multiplying and multiplying them to himself, till he makes them in his own eyes bigger and higher than he sees any other man's sins to be in the world; and it is as base to see a man do otherwise, and what follows will be base (*Luke* 18:10-14). As, therefore, I said to the great sinner before, let him take heed lest he presume; I say now to the little sinner, let him take heed that he does not dissemble; for there is as great aptness in the little sinner to dissemble as there is in the great one. 'He that hideth his sins shall not prosper', be he a sinner little or great (*Prov.* 28:13).

EIGHTH, Would Jesus Christ have mercy offered, in the first place, to the biggest sinners? Then *this shows the true cause why Satan makes such head as he does against him.*

The Father and the Holy Spirit are well spoken of by all deluders and deceived persons; Christ only is the rock of offence. 'Behold, I lay in Zion a stumbling-stone and rock of offence' (*Rom.* 9:33). Not that Satan cares more for the Father or the Spirit than he cares for the Son; but he can let men alone with their notions of the Father and the Spirit, for he knows they shall never enjoy the Father or the Spirit if indeed they receive not the merits of the Son. 'He that hath the Son, hath life; he that hath not the Son of God hath not life', however they may boast themselves of the Father and the Spirit (*1 John* 5:12). Again, 'Whosoever transgresseth, and abideth not in the doctrine of Christ, hath not God. He that abideth in the doctrine of Christ, he hath both the Father and the Son'(*2 John* 9). Christ, and Christ only, can make us able to enjoy God with life and joy to all eternity. Hence he calls himself the way to the Father, the true and living way (*John* 14:6). For we cannot come to the Father but by him (*Heb.* 10:19–20). Satan knows this, therefore he hates him. Deluded persons are ignorant of this, and so they are led by the nose up and down by Satan as much as they are.

There are many things by which Satan has taken occasion to increase his rage against Jesus Christ, as, first, his love to man, and then, the many expressions of that love. He has taken man's nature upon him; he has in that nature fulfilled the law to bring in righteousness for man; and has spilt his blood for the reconciling of man to God; he has broken the neck of death, put away sin, destroyed the works of the devil, and got into his own hands the keys of death; and all these are heinous things to Satan. He cannot abide Christ for this. Besides, Christ has eternal life in himself, and that to bestow upon us; and we in all likelihood are to possess the very places from which the Satans by transgression fell, if not places more glorious. Wherefore he must needs be angry. And is it not a vexatious thing to him that we should be admitted to the throne of grace by Christ, while he stands bound over in chains of darkness to answer for his rebellions against God and his Son, at the terrible day of judgment? Yea, we, poor dust and ashes, must become his judges and triumph over him for ever: and all this on account of Jesus Christ; for he is the meritorious cause of all this.

Now though Satan seeks to be revenged for this, yet he knows it is in vain to attack the Person of Christ; he [Christ] has overcome him; therefore he [Satan] tampers with a company of silly men, that he may vilify Christ by them. And they, bold fools as they are, will not spare to spit in his face. They will rail at his person, and deny the very being of it; they will rail at his blood, and deny the merit and worth of it. They will deny the very end for which he accomplished the law, and by devices, and tricks, and quibbles, which Satan helps them to, they set up fond names and images in his place, and give the glory of a Saviour to them. Thus Satan works under the name of Christ; and his ministers under the name of the ministers of righteousness; and by his wiles and stratagems he undoes a world of men.

But there is a seed, and they shall serve him, and it shall be counted to the Lord for a generation (*Psa.* 22:30). These shall see their sins, and that Christ is the way to happiness. These shall venture themselves, both body and soul, upon his worthiness. All this Satan knows, and therefore his rage is kindled the more. Wherefore, according to his ability and allowance, he assaults, tempts, abuses, and stirs up what he can to be hurtful to these poor people, that he may, while his time shall last, make it as hard and difficult for them to go to eternal glory as he can.

Oftentimes he abuses them with wrong apprehensions of God, and with wrong apprehensions of Christ. He also casts them into the mire, to the reproach of religion, the shame of their brethren, the derision of the world, and the dishonour of God. He holds our hands while the world buffets us; he puts bearskins upon us, and then sets the dogs at us. He bedaubs us with his own foam, and then tempts us to believe that bedaubing comes from ourselves.

Oh! the rage and the roaring of this lion, and the hatred that he manifests against the Lord Jesus, and against them that are purchased with his blood! But yet, in the midst of all this, the Lord Jesus sends forth his heralds to proclaim in the nations his love to the world, and to invite them to come in to him for life. Yea, his invitation is so large that it offers his mercy in the first place to the biggest sinners of every age, which augments the devil's rage the more. Wherefore, as I said before, fret he, fume he, the Lord Jesus will 'divide the spoil' with this great one; yea, he shall divide the spoil with the strong, 'because he hath poured out his soul unto death, and he was numbered with the transgressors; and he bare the sin of many, and made intercession for the transgressors' (*Isa.* 53:12).

NINTH, Would Jesus Christ have mercy offered, in the first place, to the biggest sinners? *Let the tempted harp upon this string for their help and consolation.*

The tempted, wherever he dwells, always thinks himself the biggest sinner, the one most unworthy of eternal life. This is Satan's master argument: 'You are a horrible sinner, a hypocrite, one that has a profane heart, and one that is an utter stranger to a work of grace.' I say this is his maul, his club, his masterpiece; he does with this as some do with their most enchanting songs, he sings it everywhere. I believe there are but few saints in the world that have not had this temptation sounding in their ears. But were they only aware, Satan by all this does but drive them to the gap out at which they should go, and so escape his roaring. Says he, 'You are a great sinner, a horrible sinner, a profane-hearted wretch, one that cannot be matched for a vile one in the country.' And all this while Christ says to his ministers, Offer mercy, in the first place, to the biggest sinners. So that this temptation drives you directly into the arms of Jesus Christ.

Were therefore the tempted but aware, he might say, 'Aye, Satan, so I am, I am a sinner of the biggest size, and therefore have most need of Jesus Christ; yea, because I am such a wretch, therefore Jesus Christ calls me; yea, he calls me first; the first proffer of the gospel is to be made to the Jerusalem sinner; I am he, wherefore stand back, Satan; make a lane, my right is first to come to Jesus Christ.' This now would be like for like. This would foil the devil; this would make him say, I must not deal with this man thus; for then I put a sword into his hand to cut off my head. And this is the meaning of Peter, when he says, 'Whom resist stedfast in the faith' (*1 Pet.* 5:9). And of Paul when he says, 'Take the shield of faith, wherewith ye shall be able to quench all the fiery darts of the wicked' (*Eph.* 6:16).

Why is it said, Begin at Jerusalem, if the Jerusalem sinner is not to have the benefit of it? And if I am to have the benefit of it, let me call it to mind when Satan haunts me with continual remembrance of my sins, of my Jerusalem sins. Satan and my conscience say I am the biggest sinner; Christ offers mercy, in the first place, to the biggest sinners! Nor is the manner of the offer other than such as suits with my mind. I am sorry for my sin; yea, sorry at my heart that ever sinful thought did enter, or find the least entertainment in my wicked mind: and might I obtain my wish, I would that my heart should never more be a place for ought but the grace, and spirit, and faith of the Lord Jesus. I speak not this to lessen my wickedness; I would not for all the world but be placed by mine own conscience in the very front of the biggest sinners, that I might be one of the first that are beckoned by the gracious hand of Jesus the Saviour to come to him for mercy.

Well, sinner, you now speak like a Christian; only say thus, in a strong spirit, in the hour of temptation, and then you will, to your commendation and comfort, quit yourself well. This improving of Christ in dark hours is the life, though the hardest part, of our Christianity. We should neither stop at darkness nor at the raging of our lusts, but go on in a way of venturing, and casting the whole of our affairs for the next world at the foot of Jesus Christ. This is the way to make the darkness light, and also to allay the raging of corruption.

The first time the Passover was eaten was in the night; and when Israel took courage to go forward, though the sea stood in their way like a devouring gulf, and the host of the Egyptians followed at their heels; yet the sea gave place, and their enemies were as still as a stone till they were gone over (*Exod.* 12:8; 14:13–14, 21–22; 15:16).

There is nothing like faith to help at a pinch; faith dissolves doubts as the sun drives away the mists. And that you may not be put out, know that your time, as I said, of believing is *always*. There are times when some graces may be out of use, but there is no time wherein faith can be said to be so. Wherefore, faith must be always in exercise. Faith is the eye, is the mouth, is the hand, and one of these is of use all day long. Faith is to see, to receive, to work, or to eat; and a Christian should be seeing, or receiving, or working, or feeding all day long. Let it rain, let it blow, let it thunder, let it lighten, a Christian must still believe. At 'what time', said the good man, 'I am afraid, I will trust in thee' (*Psa.* 56:2–3).

Nor can we have a better encouragement to do this than is, by the text, set before us; even an open heart for a Jerusalem sinner. And if for a Jerusalem sinner to come, then for such a one when come. If for such a one to be saved, then for such a one that is saved. If for such a one to be pardoned his great transgressions, then for such a one who is pardoned these to come daily to Jesus Christ too, to be cleansed and set free from his common infirmities, and from the iniquities of his holy things. Therefore, let the poor sinner that would be saved labour for skill to make the best improvement of the grace of Christ to help him against the temptations of the devil and his sins.

TENTH, Would Jesus Christ have mercy offered, in the first place, to the biggest sinners? *Let those men consider this that have, or may, in a day of trial, spoken or done what their profession or conscience told them they should not, and that have the guilt and burden thereof upon their consciences.*

Whether a thing be wrong or right, guilt may pursue him that doth contrary to his conscience. But suppose a man should deny his God, or his Christ, or relinquish a good profession, and be under the real guilt thereof, shall he, therefore, conclude he is gone for ever? Let him come again with Peter's tears, and no doubt but he shall obtain Peter's forgiveness; for the text includes the biggest sinners. And it is observable that before this clause was put into this commission, Peter was pardoned his horrible revolt from his Master. He that revolts in the day of trial, if he is not shot quite dead upon the place, but is sensible of his wound, and calls out for a surgeon, shall find his Lord at hand to pour wine and oil into his wounds, that he may again be healed, and to encourage him to think that there may be mercy for him. Besides what we find recorded of Peter, you read in the Acts that some were, through the violence of their trials, compelled to blaspheme, and yet are called saints (*Acts* 26:9–11).

Hence you have a promise or two that speak concerning such kind of men, to encourage us to think that at least some of them shall come back to the Lord their God. 'Shall they fall', saith he, 'and not arise? Shall he turn away, and not return?' (*Jer.* 8:4). And, 'In that day will I assemble her that halteth, and I will gather her that is driven out, and her that I have afflicted. And I will make her that halted a remnant, and her that was cast far off a strong nation; and the LORD shall reign over them in mount Zion . . . for ever' (*Mic.* 4:6–7; see *Zeph.* 3:19). What we are to understand by 'her that halteth' is best expressed by the prophet Elijah (*1 Kings* 18:21).

I will conclude, then, that for them that have halted, or may halt, the Lord has mercy in the bank, and is willing to accept them if they return to him again. Perhaps they may never be after that of any great esteem in the house of God, but if the Lord will admit them to favour and for-giveness, O exceeding and undeserved mercy (see *Ezek.* 44:10–14)! You, then, that may be the man, remember this, that there is mercy also for you. Return, therefore, to God, and to his Son, who has yet more in store for you, and who will do you good.

But perhaps you will say, 'He does not save all revolters, and, therefore, perhaps not me.' I answer, Are you return-ing to God? If you are returning, you are the man. 'Return, ye backsliding children, and I will heal your backslidings' (*Jer.* 3:22).

Some, as I said, that revolt, are shot dead upon the place; and as for them, who can help them? But for those that cry out of their wounds, it is a sign that they are yet alive and, if they use the means in time, doubtless they may be healed.

Christ Jesus has bags of mercy that were never yet broken open or unsealed. Hence it is said that he has goodness laid up, things reserved in heaven for his. And if he breaks open one of these bags, who call tell what he can do? Hence his love is said to be such as passes knowledge, and his riches to be unsearchable. He has, nobody knows what, for nobody knows whom! He has that by him in store for such as seem, in the view of all men, to be gone beyond recovery. For this, the text is plain. What man or angel could have thought that the Jerusalem sinners were not beyond the possibility of enjoying life and mercy? Had you seen their actions, and what horrible things they did to the Son of God; yea, how stoutly they backed what they did with resolves and endeavours to persevere, when they had killed his person, against his name and doctrine; and that there was not found among them all that while, as we read of, the least remorse or regret for their doings; could you have imagined that mercy would ever have taken hold of them, at least so soon? Nay, that they, of all the world, should be counted those alone meet to have it offered to them in the very first place! For so my text commands, saying, Preach repentance and remission of sins among all nations, beginning at Jerusalem.

I tell you the thing is a wonder, and must for ever stand for a wonder among the sons of men. It stands, also, for an everlasting invitation and allurement to the biggest sinners to come to Christ for mercy. Now since, in the opinion of all men, the revolter is such a one; if he has, as I said before, any life in him, let him take encouragement to come again, that he may live by Christ.

ELEVENTH, Would Jesus Christ have mercy offered, in the first place, to the biggest sinners? *Then let God's ministers tell them so.*

There is a proneness in us, I know not how it comes about, when we are converted to despise those that are left behind. Poor fools as we are, we forget that we ourselves were so (*Titus* 3:2–3).

But would it not become us better, since we have tasted that the Lord is gracious, so to behave towards them as to give them convincing ground to believe that we have found that mercy which also sets open the door for them to come and partake with us? Ministers, I say, should do this, both by their doctrine, and in all other respects. Austerity doth not become us, neither in doctrine nor in conversation. We ourselves live by grace; let us give as we receive, and labour to persuade our fellow-sinners, which God has left behind us, to follow after, that they may partake with us of grace. We are saved by grace; let us live like them that are gracious. Let all our things, to the world, be done in charity towards them; pity them, pray for them, be familiar with them, for their good. Let us lay aside our foolish, worldly, carnal grandeur; let us not walk the streets, and have such behaviours as signify we are scarce for touching the poor ones that are left behind; no, not with a pair of tongs. It becomes not ministers thus to do.

Ministers, remember your Lord, he was familiar with publicans and sinners to a proverb: 'Behold a man gluttonous, and a wine-bibber, a friend of publicans and sinners' (*Matt.* 11:19). The first part, concerning his glut-tonous eating and drinking, to be sure, was a horrible slander; but for the other, nothing was ever spoken truer of him by the world. Now, why should we lay hands cross on this text; that is, choose good victuals, and love the sweet wine, better than the salvation of the poor publi-can? Why not be familiar with sinners, provided we hate their spots and blemishes, and seek that they may be healed of them? Why not be companionable with our carnal neighbours, if we do take occasion to do so, that we may drop, and be yet distilling some good doctrine upon their souls? Why not go to the poor man's house, and give him a penny, and a Scripture to think upon? Why not send for the poor to fetch away, at least, the fragments of your table, that the heart of your fellow-sinner may be refreshed as well as yours?

Ministers should be exemplary; but I am an inferior man, and must beware of too much meddling. But if I might, I would meddle with them, with their wives, and with their children too. I mean not this of all, but of them that deserve it, though I may not name them. But, I say, let ministers follow the steps of their blessed Lord, who, by word and deed, showed his love to the salvation of the world, in such a carriage as declared him to prefer their salvation before his own private concern. For we are com-manded to follow his steps 'who did no sin, neither was guile found in his mouth'.

And as I have said concerning ministers, so I say to all my brethren, So act that all the world may see that indeed you are the sons of love. Love your Saviour; yea, show one to another that you love him, not only by a seeming love of affection, but with the love of duty. Practical love is best. Many love Christ with nothing but the lick of the tongue. Alas! Christ Jesus the Lord must not be put off thus; 'He that hath my commandments, and keepeth them', says he, 'he it is that loveth me' (*John* 14:21).

Practical love, which stands in self-denial, in charity to my neighbour, and a patient enduring of affliction for his name – this is counted love. Right love to Christ is that which carries in it a provoking argument to others of the brethren (*Heb.* 10:24).

If a man should ask me how he might know that he loves the children of God, the best answer I could give him would be in the words of the apostle John: 'By this', says he, 'we know that we love the children of God, when we love God, and keep his commandments' (*1 John* 5:2). Love to God and Christ is then shown when we are tender of his name; and then we show ourselves tender of his name when we are afraid to break any of the least of his commandments. And when we are here, then we show our love to our brother also.

4

Conclusion, and Answers
to Objections

Now, we have obligation sufficient thus to love in that our Lord loved us, and gave himself for us, to deliver us from death, that we might live through him. The world, when they hear the doctrine that I have asserted and handled in this little book, to wit, that *Jesus Christ would have mercy offered, in the first place, to the biggest sinners,* will be apt, because they themselves are unbelievers, to think that this is a doctrine that leads to looseness, and that gives liberty to the flesh; but if you that believe love your brethren and your neighbours truly and as you should, you will put to silence the ignorance of such foolish men, and stop their mouths from speaking evil of you. And I say, let the love of Christ constrain us to this. Who deserves our heart, our mouth, our life, our goods, so much as Jesus Christ, who has bought us to himself by his blood, to this very end, that we should be a peculiar people, zealous of good works?

There is nothing more seemly in the world than to see a Christian walk as becomes the gospel; nor anything more unbecoming a reasonable creature than to hear a man say, 'I believe in Christ', and yet see in his life debauchery and profaneness. To my mind, such men should be counted the basest of men. Such men should be counted by all unworthy of the name of a Christian, and shunned by every good man, as those who are the very plague of our profession. For so it is written we should act towards them. Whoever has a form of godliness, and denies the power thereof, from such we must 'turn away' (2 *Tim.* 3:5).

It has oftentimes come into my mind to ask by what means it is that the gospel profession should be so tainted with loose and carnal gospellers. And I could never arrive at a better satisfaction in the matter than this – such men are made professors by the devil, and so put among the rest of the godly by him. A certain man had a fruitless fig tree planted in his vineyard; but by whom was it planted there? Even by him that sowed the tares, his own children, among the wheat (*Luke* 13:6; *Matt.* 13:37–40). And that was the devil.

But why does the devil act thus? Not out of love to them, but to make them offences and stumbling-blocks to others. For he knows that a loose professor in the church does more mischief to religion than ten can do that are in the world. Was it not, think you, the devil that stirred up the damsel that you read of in Acts 16 to cry out, 'These men are the servants of the most high God, which show unto us the way of salvation?' Yes it was, as is evident; for Paul was grieved to hear it. But why did the devil stir her up to cry so but because that was the way to blemish the gospel, and to make the world think that it came from the same hand as did her soothsaying and witchery (verses 16–18)? 'Holiness becometh thine house, O LORD, for ever' (*Psa.* 93:5) Therefore, whoever professes the name of Christ, let him take heed that he does not turn that profession which he makes of him into a scandal, since he has so graciously offered us, as sinners of the biggest size, in the first place, his grace to save us.

Having thus far spoken of the riches of the grace of Christ, and of the freeness of his heart to embrace the Jerusalem sinners, it may not be amiss to give you also, as a caution, an intimation of one thing, namely, that *this grace and freeness of his heart is limited to a time and day.* Whoever delays beyond the time shall perish notwithstanding. For as a king who, of grace, sends out to his rebellious people an offer of pardon, if they will accept it by a certain day, yet beheads or hangs those that come not in for mercy until the day or time is past, so Christ Jesus has set the sinner a day, a day of salvation, an acceptable time; but he who stands out, or goes on in rebellion beyond that time, is likely to come off with the loss of his soul (*2 Cor.* 6:2; *Heb.* 3:13–19; 4:7; *Luke* 19:41–42). Therefore, since things are thus, it may be convenient here to touch a little upon these particulars.

First, that this day or time thus limited, when considered with reference to this or that man, is oftentimes undiscerned by the person concerned therein, and the end of it is always kept secret. And in the wisdom of God this is so that no man, when called upon, should put off turning to God to another time. Now, and TODAY, is that and only that which is revealed in Holy Writ (*Psa.* 50:22; *Eccles.* 12:1; *Heb.* 3:13,15). And this shows us the desperate hazards which those men run who, when invitation or conviction attends them, put off turning to God to be saved till another and, as they think, a more fit season and time. For many, by so doing, defer to do this till the day of God's patience and longsuffering is ended; and then for their prayers and cries after mercy, they receive nothing but mocking, and are laughed at by the God of heaven (*Prov.* 1:20–30; *Isa.* 65:12–16; 64:4; *Zech.* 7:11–13).

Secondly, another thing to be considered is this, namely, That the day of God's grace with some men begins sooner, and also ends sooner, than it does with others. Those at the first hour of the day had their call sooner than they who were called upon to turn to God at the sixth hour of the day; yea, and those who were hired at the third hour had their call sooner than those who were called at the eleventh (*Matt.* 20:1–6).

1. The day of God's patience began with *Ishmael*, and also ended, before he was twenty years old. At thirteen years of age he was circumcised; the next year after, Isaac was born; and then Ishmael was fourteen years old. Now, the day that Isaac was weaned, that day was Ishmael rejected; and suppose that Isaac was three years old

before he was weaned, that was only the seventeenth year of Ishmael; wherefore the day of God's grace was soon ended with him (*Gen.* 17:25; 21:2–11; *Gal.* 4:30).

2. *Cain's* day ended with him early; for, after God had rejected him, he lived to beget many children, and build a city, and to do many other things. But, alas! all that while he was a fugitive and a vagabond. Nor carried he anything with him after the day of his rejection was come, but this doleful language in his conscience, 'From God's face shall I be hid' (*Gen.* 4:14).

3. *Esau*, through his excesses, would needs go sell his birthright, having no doubt, like other confident fools, that the blessing would still be his. After this he lived many years; but all of them under the wrath of God, as was, when the time came, made to appear to his destruction; for, 'when he would have inherited the blessing, he was rejected, for he found no place of repentance, though he sought it carefully with tears' (*Heb.* 12:16–17).

Many instances might be given of such tokens of the displeasure of God against such as fool away, as the wise man has it, the prize which is put into their hand (*Prov.* 17:16).

Let these things, therefore, be a further caution to those that sit under the glorious sound of the gospel and hear of the riches of the grace of God in Christ to poor sinners. To slight grace, to despise mercy, and to stop the ear when God speaks, when he speaks such great things so much to our profit, is a great provocation. He offers, he calls, he woos, he invites, he prays, he beseeches us in this day of his grace to be reconciled to him; yea, he has provided for us the means of reconciliation himself. Now, if this is despised, it must needs be provoking; and it is a fearful thing to fall into the hands of the living God.

OBJECTION: But some man may say unto me, 'Happily I would be saved, gladly I would be saved by Christ; but I fear this day of grace is past, and that I shall perish, notwithstanding the exceeding riches of the grace of God.'

ANSWER: To this doubt I would answer several things, 1. With respect to *this day*. 2. With respect to *your desires*. 3. With respect to *your fears*.

1. With respect to *this day*, that is, whether it be ended with a man or not.

i. Are you jogged, and shaken, and molested at the hearing of the Word? Is your conscience awakened and convinced then that you are at present in a perishing state, and that you have need to cry to God for mercy? This is a hopeful sign that this day of grace is not past with you. For, usually, those that are past grace, are also, in their conscience, 'past feeling', being 'seared with a hot iron' (*Eph.* 4:18–19; *1 Tim.* 4:1–2). Consequently, those past grace must be such as are denied the awakening fruits of the Word preached. The dead that hear, says Christ, shall live; at least, Christ has not quite done with them; the day of God's patience is not at an end with them (*John* 5:25).

ii. Are there, in your more private times, arguings, struggles, and strivings with your spirit to persuade you of the vanity of what vain things you love and to win you in your soul to a choice of Christ Jesus and his heavenly things? Take heed and rebel not, for the day of God's grace and patience will not be past with you till he says his 'Spirit shall strive no more' with you; for then the woe comes, when he shall depart from them and when he says to the means of grace, Let them alone (*Hos.* 4:17; 9:12).

iii. Are you visited in the night seasons with dreams about your state, and that you are in danger of being lost? Do you have heart-shaking apprehensions when deep sleep is upon you of hell, death, and judgment to come? These are signs that God has not wholly left you, or cast you behind his back for ever. 'For God speaketh once, yea twice, yet man perceiveth it not. In a dream, in a vision of the night, when deep sleep falleth upon men, in slumberings upon the bed; then he openeth the ears of men, and sealeth their instruction, that he may withdraw man from his purpose', his sinful purposes, 'and hide pride from man' (*Job* 33:14–17). All this while God has not left the sinner, nor is come to the end of his patience towards him, but stands, at least, with the door of grace ajar in his hand, as being loth, as yet, to bolt it against him.

iv. Are you followed with affliction, and do you hear God's angry voice in your afflictions? Does he send with the affliction an interpreter, to show you your vileness, and why, or wherefore, the hand of God is upon you, and upon what you have; to wit, that it is for your sinning against him, and that you might be turned to him? If so, your summer is not quite ended; your harvest is not yet quite over and gone. Take heed, stand out no longer, lest he cause darkness, and lest your feet stumble upon the dark mountains; and lest, while you look for light, he turn it into the shadow of death, and make it gross darkness (*Jer.* 8:20; 13:15-17).

v. Are you crossed, disappointed, and waylaid, and overthrown in all your foolish ways and doings? This is a sign God has not quite left you, but that he still waits upon you to turn you. Consider, I say: has he made a hedge and a wall to stop you? Has he crossed you in all you put your hand to? Take it as a call to turn to him; for, by his thus doing he shows he has a mind to give you a better portion. For usually, when God gives up men, and resolves to let them alone in the broad way, he gives them rope, and lets them have their desires in all hurtful things (*Hos.* 2:6-15; *Psa.* 73:3-13; *Rom.* 11:9).

Therefore take heed to this also, that you strive not against the hand of God; but betake yourself to a serious inquiry into the causes of this hand of God upon you, and incline to think it is because the Lord would have you look to that which is better than what you would satisfy yourself with. When God had a mind to make the prodigal go home to his father, he sent a famine upon him and denied him a bellyful of the husks which the swine did eat. And observe it, now that he was in a strait, he betook himself to consideration of the good that there was in his father's house; yea, he resolved to go home to his father, and his father dealt well with him; he received him with music and dancing, because he had received him safe and sound (*Luke* 15:14-32).

vi. Do you have any enticing touches of the Word of God upon your mind? Does some holy word of God as it were give a glance upon you, cast a smile upon you, let fall, though it be but one drop of its savour upon your spirit; yea, though it stays but one moment with you? O then the day of grace is not past! The gate of heaven is not shut! Nor are God's heart and bowels withdrawn from you as yet. Take heed, therefore, and beware that you make much of the heavenly gift, and of that good Word of God which he has made you taste. Beware, I say, and take heed; there may be a falling away for all this; but, I say, as yet God has not left you, as yet he has not cast you off (*Heb.* 6:1–9).

2. With respect to *your desires,* what are they? Would you be saved? Would you be saved with a thorough salvation? Would you be saved from guilt and filth too? Would you be the servant of your Saviour? Are you indeed weary of the service of your old master the devil, sin, and the world? And have these desires put your soul to flight? Have you, through desires, betaken yourself to your heels? Do you fly to him that is a Saviour from the wrath to come, for life?

If these are your desires, and if they are unfeigned, fear not! You are one of those runaways whom God has commanded our Lord to receive, and not to send you back to the devil, your master, again but to give you a place in his house, even the place which you like best. 'Thou shalt not deliver unto his master', says he, 'the servant which is escaped from his master unto thee. He shall dwell with thee, even among you, in that place which he shall choose in one of your gates, where it liketh him best: you shalt not oppress him' (*Deut.* 23:15–16).

This is a command to the church, consequently to the Head of the church; for all commands from God come to her through her Head. Whence I conclude, that as Israel of old was to receive the runaway servant who escaped from a heathen master to them, and should not dare to send him back to his master again; so Christ's church now, and consequently Christ himself, may not, will not, refuse that soul that has made his escape from sin, Satan, the world, and hell, unto him, but will certainly let him dwell in his house, among his saints, in that place which he shall choose, even where he likes best.

For he says, in another place, 'And him that cometh to me, I will in no wise cast out.' In no wise, let his crimes be what they will, either for nature, multitude, or the attendance of aggravating circumstance. Wherefore, if your desires be firm, sound, and unfeigned to become the saved of Christ, and his servant, fear not, he will not, he will *in no wise* put you away, or turn you over to your old master again.

3. As to *your fears,* whatever they are, let that be supposed which is supposed before and they are groundless, and so of no weight.

OBJECTION: 'But I am afraid I am not [of the] elect, or chosen to salvation, though you called me fool a little before for so fearing.'

Answer: Though election is, in order, before calling, as to God, yet the knowledge of calling must go before the belief of my election, as to myself. Wherefore souls that doubt of the truth of their effectual calling do but plunge themselves into a deeper labyrinth of confusion that concern themselves with their election; I mean, while they labour to know it before they prove their calling. 'Make your calling, and [so your] election sure' (2 *Pet.* 1:4–10).

Wherefore, at present, lay the thoughts of your election by, and ask yourself these questions: Do I see my lost condition? Do I see that salvation is nowhere but in Christ? Would I share in this salvation by faith in him? And would I, as was said before, be thoroughly saved, to wit, from the filth as from the guilt? Do I love Christ, his Father, his saints, his words, and ways? This is the way to prove we are elect. Wherefore, sinner, when Satan, or your own heart, seeks to puzzle you with election, say you, I cannot attend to talk of this point now, but stay till I know that I am called of God to the fellowship of his Son, and then I will show you that I am elect, and that my name is written in the book of life.

If poor distressed souls would observe this order, they might save themselves the trouble of an unprofitable labour under these unseasonable and soul-sinking doubts.

Let us, therefore, upon the sight of our wretchedness, fly and venturously leap into the arms of Christ, which are now as open to receive us into his bosom as they were when nailed to the cross. This is coming to Christ for life aright; this is the right running away from your [old] master to him, as was said before. And for this we have multitudes of Scriptures to support, encourage, and comfort us in our so doing.

But now, let him that does this be sure to look for it, for Satan will be with him tomorrow to see if he can get him again to his old service; and if he cannot do that, then will he enter into dispute with him, to wit, about whether he is elect to life, and called indeed to partake of this Christ, to whom he is fled for succour, or whether he comes to him of his own presumptuous mind. Therefore we are bid, as to come, so to arm ourselves with that armour which God has provided that we may resist, quench, stand against, and withstand all the fiery darts of the devil (*Eph.* 6:11–18). If, therefore, you find Satan in this order to march against you, remember that you had this advice about it; and betake yourself to faith and good courage, and be sober, and hope to the end.

OBJECTION: 'But how if I should have sinned the sin unpardonable, or that called the sin against the Holy Ghost?'

ANSWER: If you have, you are lost for ever; but yet before it is concluded by you that you have so sinned, know that those that would be saved by Jesus Christ, through faith in his blood, cannot be counted for such.

1. *Because of the promise,* for that must not be frustrated, and it says, 'Him that cometh to Christ he will in no wise cast out.' And again, 'Whosoever will, let him take the water of life freely' (*John* 6:37; *Rev.* 21:6; 22:17).

But, I say, how can these Scriptures be fulfilled, if he that would indeed be saved, as before said, has sinned the sin unpardonable? The Scriptures must not be made void, nor their truth be cast to the ground. Here is a promise, and here is a sinner; a promise that says he shall not be cast out that comes; and the sinner comes, wherefore he must be received. Consequently, he that comes to Christ for life, has not, cannot have sinned that sin for which there is no forgiveness. And this might suffice for an answer to any coming soul that fears, though he comes, that he has sinned the sin against the Holy Ghost.

2. But, again, he that has sinned the sin against the Holy Ghost *cannot come, has no heart to come, can by no means be made willing to come to Jesus Christ for life;* because he has received such an opinion of him, and of his things, as deters and holds him back.

i. He counts this blessed person, this Son of God, a magician, a conjuror, a witch, or one that did what he did, when he was in the world, by the power and spirit of the devil (*Matt.* 9:34; 12:24–25, etc.; *Mark.* 3:22–30). Now he that has this opinion of this Jesus cannot be willing to cast himself at his feet for life, or to come to him as the only way to God and to salvation.

And hence it is said again that such a one puts him to open shame, and treads him under foot; that is, by contemning, reproaching, vilifying, and despising him, as if he were the vilest one, or the greatest cheat in the world; and has, therefore, as to his esteem of him, called him accursed, crucified him to himself, or counted him one hanged, as one of the worst of malefactors (*Heb*. 6:6; 10:29; *1 Cor*. 12:3).

ii. His blood, which is the meritorious cause of man's redemption, even the blood of the everlasting covenant, he counteth 'an unholy thing', or that which has no more virtue in it to save a soul from sin than has the blood of a dog (*Heb*. 10:29). For when the apostle says he 'counts it an unholy thing', he means, he makes it of less value than that of a sheep or cow, which were clean according to the law; and, therefore, must mean, that his blood was of no more worth to him, in his account, than was the blood of a dog, an ass, or a swine, which always was, as to sacrifices, rejected by the God of heaven, as unholy or unclean. Now he who has no better esteem of Jesus Christ, and of his death and blood, will not be persuaded to come to him for life, or to trust in him for salvation.

iii. But further, all this must be done against manifest tokens to prove the contrary, or after the shining of gospel light upon the soul, or some considerable profession of him as the Messiah, or that he was the Saviour of the world.

a. It must be done against manifest tokens to prove the contrary; and thus the reprobate Jews committed it when they saw the works of God, which put forth themselves in him, and called them the works of the devil and Beelzebub.

b. It must be done against some shining light of the gospel upon them. And thus it was with Judas, and with those who, after they were enlightened, and had tasted, and had felt something of the powers of the world to come, fell away from the faith of him, and put him to open shame and disgrace (*Heb.* 6:5–6).

c. It must also be done after, and in opposition to, one's own open profession of him. For if, after they have escaped the pollution of the world, through the knowledge of our Lord and Saviour Jesus Christ, they are again entangled therein, and overcome, the latter end is worse with them than the beginning; for it had been better for them not to have known the way of righteousness than, after they have known it, to turn from the holy commandment (which is the Word of faith) delivered unto them.

d. All this must be done openly, before witnesses, in the face, sight, and view of the world, by word and act. This is the sin that is unpardonable; and he that has thus done, can never, it is impossible he ever should, be renewed again to repentance, and that for a double reason; first, such a one says he will not; and [second], of him God says that he shall not have the benefit of salvation by him.

OBJECTION: 'But if this be the sin unpardonable, why is it called the sin against the Holy Ghost, and not rather the sin against the Son of God?'

ANSWER: It is called 'the sin against the Holy Ghost', because such count the works he did, which were done by the Spirit of God, the works of the spirit of the devil. Also because all such as so reject Christ Jesus the Lord, they do it in despite of that testimony which the Holy Ghost has given of him in the Holy Scriptures; for the Scriptures are the breathing of the Holy Ghost, as in all other things, so in that testimony they bear of the Person, of the works, sufferings, resurrection, and ascension of Jesus Christ.

Sinner, this is the sin against the Holy Ghost. What say you? Have you committed it? Nay, I know you have not, if you would be saved by Christ. Yea, it is impossible that you should have done it, if indeed you would be saved by him. No man can desire to be saved by him whom he yet judges to be an impostor, a magician, a witch. No man can hope for redemption by that blood which he yet counts an unholy thing. Nor will God ever suffer such a one to repent who has, after light and profession of him, thus horribly, and devil-like, contemned and trampled upon him.

It is true, words, and wars, and blasphemies against this Son of man are pardonable; but then they must be done 'ignorantly, and in unbelief'. Also, all blasphemous thoughts are likewise such as may be passed by, if the soul afflicted with them indeed is sorry for them (*1 Tim.* 1:13–15; *Mark* 3:28).

All but this, sinner, all but this! If God had said he would forgive one sin, it had been undeserved grace; but when he says he will pardon all but one, this is grace to the height. Nor is that one unpardonable otherwise but because the Saviour that should save them is rejected and put away. Jacob's ladder – Christ is Jacob's ladder that reaches up to heaven; and he that refuses to go there by this ladder will scarce by other means get up so high.

There is 'none other name given under heaven, among men, whereby we must be saved'. There is no other sacrifice for sin than this. He also, and he only, is the Mediator that reconciles men to God. And, sinner, if you would be saved by him, his benefits are yours; yea, though you are a great and Jerusalem transgressor.

Analysis

Chapter 1: THE TEXT EXPLAINED

LUKE 24:47: Repentance and remission of sins to be preached in all nations, 'beginning at Jerusalem'.

    i. What Jerusalem then was.
    ii. What it was to preach the gospel to them.

The observation follows: *Jesus Christ would have mercy offered, in the first place, to the biggest sinners* – This was the practice:

    i. of Christ in the Gospels.
    ii. of his apostles in Acts 1–6.

Chapter 2: WHY MERCY IS FIRST OFFERED TO THE BIGGEST SINNERS

1. Because they have the greatest need.
2. Because, when they receive it, this brings most fame to Christ's Name.
3. Because others, hearing of it, will be the more encouraged to come to Christ.

4. Because this most weakens the kingdom of Satan.

5. Because, when converted, the biggest sinners are the biggest helps to the tempted and the weak.

6. Because, when converted, they are apt to love Christ most.

7. Because grace finds more matter to kindle on in them than in other sinners.

8. Because the impenitent will be left all the more without excuse.

Chapter 3: THE DOCTRINE APPLIED

If Christ would have mercy offered first to the biggest sinners –

1. This shows us how to judge rightly of Christ's gracious intentions towards men.

2. This shows us the sufficiency of the merits of Christ to save the worst sinners.

3. This gives encouragement to those who think their sins are too great to be forgiven.

4. This gives arguments to use with unconcerned sinners to urge them to come to Christ.

5. This shows the unreasonableness of despairing of mercy.

6. This affords a warning against presumption.

7. This gives a warrant for 'little' sinners to come to Christ for mercy. 'Great' and 'little' sinners distinguished.

8. This explains the malice and the tactics of Satan against Christ, and against sinners.

9. This gives help and consolation to those who are tempted.

10. This gives help to those who have sinned against conscience in a time of trial.

11. This shows how ministers should behave towards sinners, and how all believers should love one another.

Chapter 4: CONCLUSION, AND ANSWERS TO OBJECTIONS

A caution concerning the ending of the day of grace.
Answers to the fear of a sinner –

1. That his day of grace is past.

2. That he is not elect.

3. That he has committed the unpardonable sin.
   What this sin is, and why it is said to be against the Spirit rather than against the Son of God.

Final encouragement to receive Christ and his benefits.